E. I. (Ezekiel I.) Barra

A Tale of Two Oceans

A New Story by an Old Californian

E. I. (Ezekiel I.) Barra

A Tale of Two Oceans
A New Story by an Old Californian

ISBN/EAN: 9783744669672

Printed in Europe, USA, Canada, Australia, Japan

Cover: Foto ©ninafisch / pixelio.de

More available books at **www.hansebooks.com**

NEW STORY BY AN OLD CALIFORNIAN.

JUAN FERNANDEZ.

An Account of a Voyage from Philadelphia to San Francisco,
Around Cape Horn, Years 1849-50, calling at Rio de
Janeiro, Brazil, and at Juan Fernandez,
In the South Pacific.

BY E. I. BARRA,
San Francisco, 1893.

Entered according to Act of Congress, in the year 1893, by

E. I. BARRA,

In the Office of the Librarian of Congress at Washington.

SAN FRANCISCO, 1893:
Press of Eastman & Co.

DEDICATORY.

TO WM. J. YOUNGER, M. D.

Knowing by long acquaintance with you that you like a good story, when it is modestly told, and feeling that your approbation will be a harbinger of success, I dedicate this book to you.

If in reading it you find among its pages anything to approve, or anything that will cause a smile to overspread your good natured countenance, I will feel that the reading public will not lay aside my book with a feeling of disdain or despise me for my presumption in daring to write it.

If you note the paucity of sky-scraping words, or the absence of moon-raking metaphor in this story, I hope you will find instead an appropriateness of expression and a clearness of meaning that will more than make up for the lack of "words of learnéd length and thund'ring sound," such as the schoolmaster of Goldsmith used to display with so much pride that he was a scholar of exceptional erudition.

With a sincere wish that your life may be illumined with a continuous sunshine of prosperity, I remain your friend,

THE AUTHOR.

PREFACE.

In writing and presenting this book for the entertainment of the public, I am carrying out a long cherished desire. During my eventful trip from Philadelphia to San Francisco, I wrote a diary, in which I noted all my experiences and all events that passed under my observation. When I refer to my log, as the sea diary is called, my memory is refreshed to such a degree as to make that which took place more than forty years ago seem as though it were but yesterday.

The reason why I have delayed this long contemplated wish is because of the necessary daily battle of life to win the wherewith to buy the bread and the butter to sustain the body in a working condition. Now that I have retired, like the "little bee," into winter quarters, I have taken great pleasure in recounting the stirring events of the days of '49 and '50. With this explanation I submit this, my humble volume, to the indulgent consideration of the reading public.

THE AUTHOR.

A Tale of Two Oceans.

FROM PHILADELPHIA AROUND CAPE HORN, IN THE YEARS 1849-50.

A True and Succinct Account of the Voyage.

To begin: From a voyage to Ireland with a load of corn for the famine-stricken people of that country, and from thence to Palermo, Sicily, where we took in a cargo of lemons, oranges and almonds, and from thence to Boston, where we arrived on the last day of February, 1849. After we had anchored in the lower harbor, the wind chopped around to the northwest and the air became so cold that by eight o'clock the following morning our vessel was inclosed in a sheet of ice, thereby cutting off all communication with the city. There we lay embargoed for eight days. At last, on the ninth day, the ice boat "R. B. Forbes," that had been under repairs for damage caused by ice, was again able to resume ice breaking, and she opened the channel, which enabled us to reach the wharf and discharge our cargo.

When we reached the wharf the first news we heard was that General Zachary Taylor had been elected President of the United States, and that gold had been discovered in California. We were informed that several vessels had already sailed for California, among them the ship "Edward Everett," on board of which vessel several of my young friends had taken passage. "And now," said my informant, "I suppose you will leave on the very next ship."

Well, when the cargo was discharged, all hands were paid off, and I took board with a Mr. Brodhead, who entertained a few seafaring men. There I met a man who had arrived in the ship "Remittance," on board of which ship he had been engaged for the two years previous collecting hides and tallow on the coast of California. He told me that ten days before they weighed anchor to leave Monterey a party of Americans had arrived from Coloma and brought with them a large quantity of gold dust, a specimen of which he had bought from them, and which he showed me in a tin box like a snuff box. I, in my utter ignorance about gold mining, asked him why he had not gone up to Coloma and gathered up two or three sacks of the precious dust and brought it home with him. He answered that he could not leave the ship, even if he had so desired; therefore he had come home in the ship, had been discharged and paid off, and now that he was free he was going to buy an outfit for gold mining, and take passage on board the first ship that was to leave for California. This person seemed to be so sincere and so sanguine that it caused me to reflect on the possibility of my going to California, and, in one grand swoop, digging up a big fortune.

The city of Boston, as well as all the adjacent towns, were alive on the subject of the California gold mines. The wharves were lined with ships, brigs, schooners, and even sloops, with big signs which bore the legend: "The first vessel for California. For freight or passage apply to So and So, Commercial street," or Broad street. Lumber already framed for houses, barrels of beef and pork, flour, and boxes of boots, shoes, and long rubber leggings for working in the water, shovels, picks and axes, in a heterogeneous mass, were being hauled by drays alongside the vessels, and all for California.

I saw two men meet and salute. Said one: "Well, Swift, are you going to California?" "No; but I am fitting out my brother Josiah with everything necessary for a trip of two years, as well as to pay his passage to San Francisco and also to furnish the money to pay his expenses to the mines, and in return I am to receive one-half of all his gains for the two years that he is to be gone."

I afterwards found that many persons in New England who had faith in the gold discoveries but could not go themselves, had adopted the plan of fitting out a relative or a reliable friend with all necessary outfit for the period of two years, paying their passage out and securing themselves for the outlay by drawing up a legal agreement, in which the adventurer bound himself to divide all that he would gain during the two years with the friend who fitted him out for the trip, share and share alike.

Many parties that were composed of from fifty to a hundred, would buy a vessel, load her with building materials and provisions, and, as the party generally had more or less sailors, they would sail her themselves, and when they arrived in San Francisco sell vessel and cargo for what they could get, and then proceed to the mines; and many companies took along small boats, which, upon their arrival in San Francisco, they provisioned and went up the Sacramento or San Joaquin rivers in their own boat.

The first ship that I saw depart for California was the "Sweden." She was lying at Lewis' wharf. The morning on which she sailed was an eventful one to the voyagers and their friends. The morning was clear and cold, with the wind northwest blowing straight out of the harbor. Everybody about the wharf and on board the ship seemed to be very busy. Baggage in great quantities was being brought down the wharf and put on board the ship. Fresh provisions were hoisted on board, such as quarters of beef, carcasses of mutton, killed and dressed hogs, cabbages, turnips and other fresh food, which gave evidence that the owners of the ship intended to treat the passengers and crew in a liberal manner. The crew of the ship were busy on board preparing for their departure, while many of the passengers were taking leave of their relatives and friends.

One group that particularly attracted my attention was composed of three persons, two ladies and a gentleman. The ladies appeared to be a mother and daughter. The gentleman was apparently about twenty-three years of age and was as fine looking a young fellow as would be seen in a day's travel. Many of the persons there had accompanied relatives from their distant homes, even as far off as New Hampshire and Vermont. Many New England mothers were there, looking every one of them a heroine that she was. They were taking leave of their darling sons for a long while at least. As I approached the group of three persons I noticed the young man clasping the hand of the young lady in his own, while her sad, tearful face was bent down to hide her grief. The elder lady spoke and said, "Cyrus, I told you a month ago, when you first told of your intention to go to California, that a steady, industrious man can win gold at home; but a good, thrifty, prudent wife he can't win every day." At this remark the young lady burst into fresh tears, which she could not keep back. The young man softly stroked her hand while he answered her mother, saying "Mrs. Hamblin, I am not in a condition just now to do as I would like to do; but after this mining trip of two years, or perhaps less time, I hope to be able to build a nice house over in Dracut, just far enough from Lowell to make it seem like the country. Then Deborah and myself will be married and settle down in a home of our own. And I intend to have a nice gentle horse and a family carryall, and she will be able to drive over to your house every fine day and take you all around the neighborhood." At this glowing description of anticipated happiness the young lady looked up at her lover and smiled pleasantly at his description of the joy to come.

This incident brought to my mind the lines of the poet Burns, wherein he says:

> "The best laid schemes o' mice and men
> Gang aft agley,
> And lea'e us naught but grief and pain
> For promised joy."

Now all those that were going were hurrying on board. The pilot went on board and ordered the mate to get everything ready for a start. The mate sung out to the men aloft,

"Drop the bunts of the fore and main top-sails." Then to the men on deck—"Sheet home!" "Now man the halyards and hoist away!" "Aye, aye, sir!" "Give us a shanter, somebody," sung out the men, at which one of the sailors struck up a hoisting song:

"Nancy Banana she married a barber!"
CHORUS.
"Haul her away, boys! Haul her away!"

"She married a barber who shaved without lather!"
CHORUS.
"Haul her away, boys! Haul her away!"

When the top-sails were mastheaded, the pilot sung out to cast off the bow line. "Now run up your jib, Mr. Mate. Now ease away on your spring line;" and the vessel began to move from the wharf. Then the pilot sung out, "Let go your spring and stern lines!" Then the good ship began to forge ahead; and the last cord that held the ship tied to the land was cast off and she was as free as the bird that flew around her masthead. Just then a number of the passengers mounted the quarter-deck and struck up a song that was then quite in vogue in minstrel exhibitions, changing a few words of the chorus to suit the occasion. It ran thus:

"I dreamt a dream the other night when everything was still;
I dreamt I saw Susanah, a coming down the hill.
She had a pancake in her mouth ; a tear was in her eye ;
Says I, ' O Susanah, dear; Susanah, don't you cry.'"
CHORUS.
"O! Susanah, don't you cry for me!
For I'm bound to California with my washbowl on my knee."

In those early days of mining the miner would fill a sack with auriferous soil, take it to the nearest rivulet of water, and wash it out in a common tin pan or washbowl, as the soil, being much lighter than the gold, would float off and leave the gold dust in the bottom of the pan.

As the ship shot out into the harbor under the impulse of the favoring breeze, three hearty cheers were given by the people on the wharf, and were answered by the departing voyagers. As the ship moved majestically down the harbor with all sail spread, she was indeed a fine spectacle. As the concourse of people began to leave the wharf to go up into the city it was very easy to pick out those persons that had taken leave of their departing friends from those that were mere spectators of the novel scene.

I owned one-quarter in a sixty-ton schooner that had been lying up all winter in New Bedford, and as I was now disengaged, I went there and arranged with the captain—who also owned a quarter in the vessel—to sail with him on shares, the other half being owned by two Boston merchants. After obtaining the consent of the other owners, we had the vessel hauled out on the marine railway, recalked and painted, and then sailed for the Capes of Virginia. We went up the Hampton Roads and into the Sansemond River, where we loaded with corn in bulk for Boston. We made this trip without any particular incident, returned to Chesapeake Bay, went up the Potomac River and loaded with corn and oats for Providence, R. I.

During all this time I was thinking about California and my young friends who had sailed for there during the month of December, and who might return by the following December loaded down with sacks of gold, thereby gaining the admiration of all the young women, and the envy of all the young men of their acquaintance.

These thoughts swayed my mind to such a degree that by the time we arrived in Providence I had made up my mind to "go to California with my washbowl on my knee." As soon as we had discharged our cargo of grain I informed the captain. He very kindly reckoned up our gains and divided with me, and wished me good luck in my new venture.

I took the cars, went to Boston, and there called upon my friends, the merchants who were owners of half the vessel, and informed them of my resolution. One of them told me that if I would make one more short trip in the schooner and the accounts from California should continue to be favorable, that he and his brother would fit the vessel out and load her with such a cargo as would find a ready market in California, and place me in command. To this generous proposition I made due acknowledgment; but I told him I would rather go to California by the Isthmus Route, so that when I arrived there I would be free legged and unconfined.

When these kind gentlemen saw that I was determined to go they bought my quarter interest in the vessel, paid me the money, and wished me good luck and bushels of gold dust.

I now prepared to start as soon as possible. I purchased an outfit such as I was told would be required, and, after taking leave of my kind friends in Boston and vicinity, I bought my ticket for New York and started one afternoon in the cars for Fall River from the Old Colony Depot. When we arrived in Fall River we embarked on the steamer "Oregon." The steamer moved down Mount Hope Bay and out into the beautiful Narragansett a-kiting. The bell now rang for dinner and I followed the crowd into the dining saloon, at the door of which stood a stalwart Ethiopian, who demanded a dollar, upon the receipt of which he permitted me to pass in. As I entered, another gentleman of the same persuasion took my ticket and escorted me to a seat at the table. The table was resplendent with chinaware, glassware, and silver casters. I was taken all aback with so much grandeur, and felt myself quite out of place, so different was it from what I had been accustomed to before on shipboard. The waiter, observing my embarrassment, took me in hand and brought me a number of well-filled plates. My hunger overcame my bashfulness and I began to eat, and continued my gustatory occupation until my stomach admonished me that it was time to stop.

When I went out on deck we were abreast of the Newport breakwater. Soon we came up with Fort Adams, and, passing it, we came up with Brenton's Reef. Then Beavertail Lighthouse on the starboard side; then came up with Point Judith, and next Watch Hill light, and entered the Long Island Sound.

I now turned into my berth and dreamed that I was in the mines and had already dug up and washed out a barrelful of shining gold dust. In the height of my rejoicing at my success I was awakened by the tramping of many feet and I arose and dressed myself and went out on deck to find that it was five o'clock A. M. and that we were just passing Blackwell's Island and heading for the North River side of New York City. We reached the wharf about six o'clock and I engaged a vehicle to take my baggage to a respectable boarding house on Roosevelt street.

After I took my breakfast I sallied out to find the office of the Pacific Mail Company, which I accomplished without any difficulty. Although I had been in New York many times before I had always belonged to some vessel and was therefore a stranger on shore. When I reached the place I found the sidewalk in front occupied by a crowd of men, and all of them conversing about California and the latest news from there. The office was on the second floor, and as I went up the stairs I found them crowded with men going up and others coming down. After I reached the office I had to wait for my turn to approach the counter. When I had accomplished this feat, sore indeed was my disappointment to learn from the agent that he could not sell me a through ticket to California. All that he could do was to sell a ticket to Chagres, from whence I could make my way to Panama, through swamps and over mountains, a distance of more than fifty miles, after which I could trust to luck to obtain passage for San Francisco, as all the tickets for cabin and steerage on the Pacific side were already sold as far off as the following December. I turned sadly from the counter and went down stairs.

When I reached the street a very respectable looking gentlemen spoke to me and asked me if I had bought my ticket. I answered that I had not. "Then," said he, "I advise you not to do so, for the reason that the Isthmus is crowded with people that can't get away. I have a fine ship that is now loading in Philadelphia for San Francisco, and I am the master and part owner of her. She will have finished loading within ten days, and we shall sail for San Francisco within two days thereafter. I am going to take my wife and only daughter with me, and that is a guarantee that the ship is sound and seaworthy. Now I will tell you: I saw you come out of the steamship office, and I like your appearance, and although I have nearly all my cabin passengers engaged, and I will take no others, I want you to go with me, and I will make a deduction in the price of passage in your favor."

He was a man of fine presence, standing six feet or over, of a florid complexion, and of an address so pleasant and friendly that he won my confidence. I, like a simpleton that I was, accepted all that he told me as honest truth. He directed me to call that evening at the Merchants' Hotel and inquire of the clerk for Capt. Blanchard. He then left me and I strolled around the wharves and saw many ships with signs out: "First vessel for California; cargo all engaged; will leave in five days. For passage only apply to so and so, Maiden Lane."

At six o'clock I went to my boarding house and ate my

supper, after which I made my way to the Merchants' Hotel and asked the clerk for Capt. Blanchard of the ship "Samson." He told me that the captain was then taking his dinner and would soon come into the reading-room. I stood around awhile and heard the gentlemen talking about ships and quick passages and so on, and I inferred that the place was the headquarters of sea captains. I stood around awhile and after a time I saw the captain enter the room. When he saw me he greeted me cordially and invited me to his room. Then he began by saying, "When I saw you this morning I was favorably impressed by your appearance, and I like your modest and manly manner. Now I'll tell you what I'll do for you. The price of passage on my ship is fixed at two hundred dollars for cabin, and there will be no steerage passengers on board, so that we may not be crowded on such a long voyage. I'll deduct one-quarter of the price in your favor, which you can pay to the ship's agent in Philadelphia, to whom you can hand the note which I will now give you. After you have paid your passage you can go aboard the ship at South street wharf and hand this note to Mr. Cranston, the mate, who will then let you pick your berth in the upper cabin, as the lower cabin is to be devoted to the use of families, who have already engaged all the staterooms." "I suppose we shall live pretty well in the cabin, Captain," I ventured to remark. "Live pretty well!" said he. "On that you may depend. As you are an old shell-back like myself I don't mind telling you all about it. I am determined that we shall live like fighting cocks. I have already engaged a half dozen coops of chickens, a large lot of ducks and a dozen of half-grown pigs, for I myself am fond of sea pie made with good fresh pig. The tables of the upper and lower cabins shall be identical. There shall be no difference. Every day for dinner there shall be plum duff, with raisins or Zante currants, and wine sauce. For a change there will be rice pudding with eggs, and I am sorry we can't carry a cow, for then we could use milk also. Also we shall have mince or dried apple pies. Why, sir, by the time that we arrive in California, in place of being as lean as a dolphin, as you are now, you'll be as fat as a porpoise."

After this pleasant interview I left the captain, feeling highly elated with my good luck, and that indeed "my lines had fallen in pleasant places." But, alas for the truth, I saw neither chickens, ducks nor half-grown pigs on board the ship "Samson" while I was on board of her, only in my mind's eye.

I returned to my boarding house and to bed, being determined to take the first train for Philadelphia the next day. I arose the next morning, walked down to the Battery and viewed the harbor with innumerable vessels moving hither and yon. I saw a Liverpool packet of the black ball line that had arrived the evening before. Her decks were black with immigrants, there were so many. At that time the only steamships that crossed the Atlantic made their port in Boston, and they took only cabin passengers, therefore the packet ships of that day were of great importance.

After looking around awhile I returned to the boarding house and ate my breakfast, after which I went to the railroad office and there learned that by taking the night slow train that the cost of passage would be much less and still I would arrive in Philadelphia quite early the following morning. I bought my ticket and walked around; went up Chatham street, the Bowery and other places that sailors used to talk about when we were at sea. At one o'clock I returned to my boarding house, ate my dinner, paid my bill and then engaged a dray to take my baggage to the Jersey City ferry.

At five o'clock we left the ferry landing and crossed to Jersey City. There we got on board the cars and about six o'clock started for Philadelphia. In the same seat with me sat an old gentleman, who asked me where I was from and where I was going. After I had answered these questions, apparently to his satisfaction, he took me into his confidence and told me that he was from Boston, where he had been engaged in business for many years and had by his industry and frugality accumulated a sum equal to seventy thousand dollars, the most of which he had invested in real estate, and he had retired from business because he felt that he had money enough. That was many years ago, and I will say that he is the only man that I ever heard make such a declaration.

He further told me that his son, who had gone to New Orleans some years ago and was now established in business, had sent him an urgent invitation to come and pass the winter with him in the genial climate of the South. He said he was then on his way by way of Cincinnati, to which place he was going by rail, and from thence by river on one of the floating palaces down the Ohio river into the great Mississippi, and down to New Orleans. After passing the winter in the company of his son and family, and spring was well advanced, he would embark on board of one of the numerous vessels that sail from New Orleans to Boston, and go home by the way of the Gulf of Mexico and the Florida Straits, until he would again reach his New England home—than which there is no sweeter spot on earth to him.

By this time it had become dark, and the lamps in the car had been lighted. The passengers, one after the other, were dropping asleep. I had the inside seat, and in the seat opposite mine sat a lady holding a child, about eighteen months' old, that had been crowing, talking baby-talk, and kicking from the time we had started, and now from sheer exhaustion it had fallen asleep in its mother's arms. The old gentleman beside me was now in the land of nod.

I was ruminating in my mind over my novel situation—so different from my usual one of a life on shipboard. I was roused from my reverie by the lady on the opposite seat saying to me: "Young man, I see that you don't seem to be either tired or sleepy, while I am both, and feel all worn out with taking care of my baby. Now will you, like a good young man as I see that you are, just hold my baby while I take a half hour of rest?" What could I say, only to answer in the affirmative, and took the child from her arms for half an hour. The mother settled herself in her seat, and for two successive hours she slept and snored at the rate of ten knots an hour.

I felt that I was doing some little good in the world, and was satisfied; when at the end of the two hours we came to a place where there was some change to be made, the lady woke up, and relieved me of my charge, with many thanks.

In the morning we arrived in Philadelphia. I left my baggage at the depot, and made my way to the Red Bank Ferry Hotel, to which place Capt. Blanchard had directed me to go. I told Mr. and Mrs. Clements that Capt. Blanchard had directed me to put up at their hotel. Mr. Clements said that Capt. Blanchard was one of their patrons whenever he was in Philadelphia. Mr. Clements showed me into a snug little room in the third story, from the one window of which I had a good view of the surrounding housetops, and could admire the steeples of the different churches.

I descended to the street and engaged a drayman to fetch my baggage from the depot.

After I had got my things into the little room, I opened my chest, took out my comb and brush, and, there being a pitcher of water and a basin in the room, I spruced up a little and went down stairs to my breakfast.

After breakfast I started out to attend to the business that had brought me to Philadelphia. I asked the way to the South street wharf, and it was pointed out to me, and I found that the ship didn't lay far from the hotel. I went on board and handed the note which the captain had given, to the mate of the ship Mr. Cranston. He read the note, and then reached out his hand to me in a friendly manner, and said that he was glad to greet me, as Capt. Blanchard said that he thought that I was a likely young man and he hoped all the other passengers, most of whom were already engaged, would prove to be as pleasant to the officers of the ship and to one another, as that would be an important matter on such a long voyage as the one we were about to enter upon.

I will here describe the mate. He was a man about five feet nine inches in height, with a round, plump face, sun-browned by the sun, entirely unshaven, a small nose surmounted by a pair of gold-rimmed spectacles, dark eyes, black curly hair and beard, and pouting, smiling lips, and apparently about thirty years of age. To me he looked like a lawyer's clerk much more than he did like a sailor. However, he was very complaisant to me, and told me that he was from Massachusetts, and had been up to that present time master of an East Indiaman; but he had determined to go to California and try his fortune in the land of gold. He said that being an old acquaintance of Capt. Blanchard he had joined his ship as first mate with the agreement that he should leave the ship when she arrived in California.

The ship "Samson" I found to be an eastern built craft of the old fashioned kettle-bottom model, built for carrying more than for speed. She had been engaged in the cotton trade, taking a cargo of cotton from New Orleans or Mobile to Liverpool, and going from there to Saint Ubes in Portugal, or Cadiz in Spain, and thence taking a cargo of salt to Bath, Me., for the use of the Grand Bank fishermen; then after painting and refitting, the ship would repeat the voyage the following year. She was what the sailors called a good old monthly ship. I could see that she was not a clipper, but she looked sound and solid and of about five hundred tons burthen.

I determined to go in her, and I asked Mr. Cranston the direction to the office of the agent. He directed me along the city front and told me the number of the house. When I arrived at the office I found Mr. Perkins, the agent, at his desk, and, bowing to him politely, I handed him the note from Captain Blanchard. After he read the note he said to me, "Are you an old acquaintance of Capt. Blanchard?" "No, sir," I answered; "I never saw him before I met him in New York." "Why I asked you is because he informs me in this note that you are to have your passage to San Francisco at one-quarter less than the regular price. However, I suppose he has his motives for so doing." I learned afterwards that Mr. Perkins was correct in his surmise.

I paid my passage, received my ticket and returned to the ship in order to select my berth. When I asked of the mate which berth I could have, he naively told me to take any one I chose. "Why, sir," I replied, "the captain told me that nearly every berth in the upper cabin was already engaged." "Well, well," said he, "I guess they are; but, you know, the agent don't keep me informed about such matters."

The upper cabin contained two staterooms aft, one of which was to be occupied by the mates; and one forward on the larboard side. On the starboard side forward was the pantry. Between the staterooms, extending the length of the cabin, were thirty berths, fifteen on each side.

The center of the cabin was occupied by a table extending its whole length. Over the table were swinging racks, which were filled with wine glasses, tumblers and highly polished casters—all very suggestive of good eating that was to come upon the table after we got started for California. The pantry was well stocked with dishes, and mutely told all intending passengers that they might expect to fare high. I afterwards learned that this was all for effect, and not for use. The lower cabin, I learned, had been engaged by a number of French families, who had been the adherents of Louis Phillip, the late king in their own country, and, after the *coup de etat* by Louis Napoleon, had left France in order to settle in Philadelphia, and try their fortunes in the new world. On hearing the wonderful accounts of the gold discoveries in California they had determined to be among the first to reach that land of fabulous wealth.

I selected my berth in the first row abaft the pantry, being nearest the cabin door, and placed a ticket on it to secure it. While I was looking around on board, four drays were driven to the ship's side and unloaded of heavy cases. After a time a number of stevedores, with their foreman, came on board and took off the hatches in order to take the goods on board. For the first time I went down into the hold, and found that the lower deck was not more than half full, while the 'tween decks had only a few cases in it. I said to the mate that it didn't look as though the ship could sail in ten days, seeing how little she had then on board.

"Well," said he; "you know that a great quantity of cargo can be stowed on board of a ship in ten days, and as the agent tells me that every ton of freight that can be stowed away is already engaged, we will, without doubt, get away from here by the last of this month, or by the first of August, sure.

That evening Mr. Clement, the landlord of the hotel, told me that the clipper brig "Tecumseh," Capt. Lyle, was receiving a quick dispatch and was nearly loaded, and had all her passengers engaged, and without doubt after she left the "Samson," being the next nearest loaded, would receive a quick dispatch.

The next morning I went to the wharf where the "Tecumseh" laid and saw that she was loaded chock-a-block, and that she had considerable freight on deck. This inspired me with the thought that our ship, being the next nearest loaded, that we would be enabled to start near the stipulated time.

I now turned my attention to buying a venture for the California market. I had been informed that pickles of all kinds were in demand by the miners, and could be sold there at a large profit. I went to "Smith's pickle preserving establishment," and bought a large quantity of pickles in glass jars, and superintended the packing in boxes in a manner that would insure their safe transportation. I also bought twenty thousand Philadelphia made cigars, which I afterwards retailed in San Francisco at twenty-five cents apiece.

After buying a few other articles that I thought would be in demand in California, I packed them into cases and sent them on board the "Samson," and obtained the bills of lading from Mr. Perkins, the agent. I didn't insure my venture for the reason that if anything happened to the ship I wouldn't have any use for the money to be recovered from the company.

After I had arranged and shipped my goods, I turned my attention to viewing the sights of the Quaker City, as it is called. I learned that it is so called because it was settled by Quakers led by William Penn, who had received a grant of land from the King of England. The State of Pennsylvania is called the Keystone State for the reason that it was the center one of the thirteen original States of the Union.

My first pilgrimage was made to that historical building, Independence Hall, where that illustrious, self-sacrificing body of patriots assembled and then pledged their fortunes and their lives for the achievement and maintenance of the freedom of this great and glorious country. To take it and to hold it free from the domination of King George the Third of England and all his cohorts. I went and viewed the hall where American Independence was born in the year 1776, and offered a silent prayer to the Ruler of Nations that this land may continue to be the land of the free and the home of the brave to the end of time.

When I returned to the hotel that evening I found two young men there waiting for me. They told me that they came from the interior of the State, and were going to California; that they had never seen a ship before, and when they went on board the "Samson" they became timid and were rather dubious about taking passage on her. Capt. Blanchard, who had returned from down East with his wife and child, had told them that he would take his family along and also referred them to me as being a sailor, and that I had engaged and paid for my passage on his ship, and told them that they would find me at the Red Bank Hotel. I told them that I thought that the "Samson" was a substantial craft, not very speedy, yet a safe vessel to go to sea in. After hearing my statement they said that they would pay their passage the following day, and they did and became my fellow-passengers on the ship.

A few days afterwards a gentleman, accompanied by his wife, came on the same kind of errand and informed me that Capt. Blanchard had referred him to me in regard to the seaworthiness of the ship. He told me that he had sold out his store in the interior of the State, and in company of his wife was going to try the climate of California for the benefit of his health as well as to improve his fortune. As to his health, his looks showed that there was plenty of room for improvement. They also became my fellow-passengers, and afterwards when he and his wife left the ship in Rio Janeiro and paid their passage to California on another ship, he mildly reproached me, saying that had it not been for me he would have waited in Philadelphia for another vessel.

I now could see the reason why Capt. Blanchard had made a quarter reduction in my passage. It was because he wanted to use me as a standing reference as to the seaworthiness of his ship, among these honest country people who had no confidence in their own judgment. And I at once determined that after that I would simply say that I knew nothing about the ship further than having paid my passage on her and intended to go in her.

I now found out that Capt. Blanchard was not a man to throw a sprat unless it would catch for him a mackerel.

The ship was slowly filling up and I thought that we might be ready to sail by the latter part of August.

After visiting the historic Independence Hall my next desire was to visit the United States Mint—the first that was established in the United States. In the year 1791 Congress passed an act establishing a national Mint in Philadelphia, the capital of the United States at that time. President Washington, it is said, took great interest in forwarding the preparations, but the progress was slow; therefore, the first coinage in the new Mint took place in 1793, in which year copper cents were coined. In the following year, October, 1794, the first American dollars were issued, since which time the American silver coins have gradually displaced the foreign silver coins with which, up to recent years, this country has been flooded. There have been several mints established since, but they are only branches, as this is the parent mint, and supplies all the others with dies and other delicate machinery.

My next visit was to Girard College. This is an educational institution established by Stephen Girard, a Philadelphia merchant of French birth, living very poor in order that he might die very rich. This institution will most certainly perpetuate his name in honor, and many an educated Philadelphian has cause to gratefully honor the name of Stephen Girard.

Philadelphia is situated at the confluence of two rivers, the Delaware and Schuylkill. One street, called Market street, extends from the bank of the Delaware river to the bank of the Schuylkill. On the Delaware side it is built with fine and substantial buildings, but as you approach the Schuylkill river the houses are wooden structures, apparently built to cover as much waste ground as possible.

When I reached the Schuylkill side I found the bank of the river occupied by schooners and sloops that were being loaded with coal from canal boats, to be carried to eastern ports. On the opposite side of the Schuylkill was a vast oozy marsh, covered with reeds, and I saw sportsmen going over in flat bottomed boats to shoot wild ducks.

I next visited Kensington, a suburb of Philadelphia, on the Delaware river, where the cars come in immense trains loaded with coal; and here I found something different from what I had ever seen before. The cars were carried on trestled tracks quite a distance over the deep part of the river, the schooners were then hauled alongside, a shoot run into her hatchway, and the bottom was dropped in each car in its turn and the coal was shot into the vessel's hold in the twinkling of an eye. It was then trimmed by lumpers, and in two hours' time a two hundred tons' schooner would be ready to go down the river fully loaded.

I contrasted this with what I had seen in other places. I once belonged to a brig that went to Pictou, Nova Scotia. When we arrived there we were ordered to a place on the opposite side of the harbor called New Glasgow, to there load with coal. With the primitive style that prevailed then it took us four days to load two hundred tons of coal, whereas I saw the schooner loaded with same quantity of coal in two hours.

Whatever the Americans have to do they do it with celerity, showing thereby that they practice the injunction of Saint Paul, wherein he says: "Whatever thy hands findeth to do, that do with all thy might."

One morning I read in the "Ledger" that there was to be a great play performed at the Walnut Street Theatre, and among other attractions there to appear, was Collins the Irish comedian and singer of songs.

I determined to attend, and immediately after supper in the evening I made my way to the theatre. The play of that night was, I think, composed by Sheridan Knowles. The leading female character came on the stage arrayed in a riding habit, with hat on head and whip in hand, and began reciting her wonderful exploits in a most rhapsodical manner, about leaping over dikes, clearing wide ditches, and other equestrian achievements. The more she talked the louder the audience clapped, until the house was in a furor of excitement; finally the actress had to withdraw from very exhaustion. At the conclusion of the piece the lady was called before the curtain and received an ovation of hearty applause. I didn't see any flowers thrown upon the stage, for at that time the practice of emptying the contents of a flower shop upon the stage did not prevail. I afterwards learned that the name of the actress was Miss Alexina Fisher, and that she was a great favorite with the people of Philadelphia. The next was to be the "grand piece de resistance," Mr. Collins the Irish comedian and songster. After a short lull the stage manager came to the footlights and announced Mr. Collins; as he uttered the name a fine looking gentleman emerged from the wings, amid the uproarious applause of the audience, alow and aloft. The actor bowed, and the people clapped until the audience seemed to have tired themselves out. Mr. Collins was a man that stood about five feet eleven inches in height, very erect, had dark curly hair, a ruddy complexion, dark eyes, and a very pleasing expression of countenance. The music struck up and Mr. Collins sang thus:

> "Oh, Widder Machree, its no wonder you frown,
> Och, hone! Widder Machree;
> It spoils your looks, that same dirty black gown,
> Och, hone! Widder Machree."

His grimaces were wonderful contortions of the human

face. At the end of each stanza, the audience would shout to the echo. To me, it seemed flat, stale, and unprofitable; but, I suppose it was very profitable to Mr. Collins, and that was all that he wanted. He seemed to please his listeners and thus put money in his purse.

After the performance I wended my way towards my hotel, and when I reached the first corner below the theatre, I heard the cry: "Hot corn! hot corn! all hot." As I approached the spot from whence the cry emanated, I found that it was a Negro woman, who was standing on the street corner, with an immense tin kettle in front of her, which was kept hot by an alcohol lamp. I saw her draw ears of boiled corn out of the kettle, and dispense them to finely dressed gentlemen, who appeared to be of the "haut ton" of Philadelphia society. They received the corn from the woman and proceeded to eat it, there and then. When they had finished, they pulled out their handkerchiefs, wiped their hands, paid the woman, and went their way, just as if it was a most common-place affair with them to do so, and as if they had been "to the manor born."

Afterwards, as the season advanced and the evenings became more cool, the green corn was succeeded by what is called pepperpot. It is composed of calveshead, fine cut tripe, sliced potatoes, and seasoned with capsicum and cloves. This feast was served in little bowls, and eaten from a spoon; and like the corn, eaten while standing. Well, I said to myself, this is the most unconventional city that I ever was in. Surely, "use makes master," as the old saying goes. The people in this city seem to eat their supper in the street, and then pick their teeth as they walk along.

One Sunday I saw a crowd of people going on board a ferry boat that was bound for Red Bank, on the New Jersey side of the Delaware river, and I took a trip also. When we arrived at the landing, I found that Red Bank comprised one large wooden building, called the hotel, and a few scattering farm houses. I soon learned why people came on Sundays when I saw an immense pile of luscious looking watermelons, and rough tables and benches around it. The crowd hurried to the feast; each one picked out a watermelon, paid for it, and fell to and ate it. I did as I saw others do. I will say, although I had eaten watermelon in Vera Cruz, where it is said they are the best in the world, that the freshly gathered melons of New Jersey excel all others. After this "fete champetre," as there was no other attraction but fields of sand and watermelon patches, I took the next boat for the city. While we were on our way back I discovered that some of our passengers had found in the hotel at Red Bank something very inspiring, as they were hilarious and somewhat noisy, but there was no trouble on board the steamer, and we returned to the city in safety. It was now verging on towards the end of September.

When I left Boston, in the middle of July, I anticipated being in California by the first of October, but, instead of that, here I was in Philadelphia, with my passage paid on board of a ship that was not yet ready to sail. I now felt the full force of the old adage that, "Hope deferred maketh the heart sick." I walked down to the ship on the first day of October, and there my eyes were gladdened by seeing a gang of riggers bending the sails and reeving the running gear. I knew that this betokened the near approach of the day of our departure for the land of gold.

That evening there was an alarm of fire sounded, and the engines were rushing through the streets at a furious rate, pulled by earnest men, to the number of about fifty men to each engine. The fire was raging along the neighborhood of Shippen street. I heard that it was the Negro quarter of the city. The firemen were volunteers—young, zealous and fearless. They worked with a will to save lives and property without any hope of compensation or reward. In the midst of their dangerous labors a shot was fired, and one of their number, who was standing on the engine directing the stream of water, fell off the engine, shot dead. The exertions of the firemen now ceased, and they directed their attention to the residents of the neighborhood. In five minutes time the residents were fleeing in every direction, seeking safety from instant death at the hands of the now infuriated firemen. The disturbance became so serious that the police, who tried to suppress it, were brushed aside like so many flies. The church bells were rung, and the Mayor read the riot act, but it availed naught, for the firemen were now frantic with rage. Finally the military was called out, and something like four squares were placed under martial law. Neither man nor vehicle was allowed to approach the interdicted quarter, and it so continued up to the day that we sailed. All this tumult seemed very strange to see in a city that was called the "City of Brotherly Love." It sounded like a misnomer to me, when I remembered that about four years before a riot was fomented in this same city which culminated in the despoilment of school houses and the firing of church edifices. I will say for myself that in my wanderings about the world I was never treated more kindly anywhere than I was in Philadelphia.

The day for our departure finally arrived, to my great delight. On this fifth day of October the South street wharf was all alive with the voyagers and their leave-taking friends. There was a large number of French gentlemen and ladies who had come to bid their compatriots a "bon voyage." The men embraced each other in a most affecting manner and the ladies rained kisses upon each other in a manner that seemed to convey to each other the ardent love they felt for their country people in this the land of their exile. As I was a mere looker-on in all this demonstration, not having any other friends than those persons with whom I had become acquainted during my two months' sojourn, I felt a sympathy for them when I saw how hard it seemed to rend the ties of long cherished friendship, perhaps never to be renewed.

About eleven o'clock the steamer came alongside and her hawsers were passed to the ship preparatory to towing her down the river. South street wharf was now crowded with friends and lookers-on. The pilot came on board and ordered the shore lines to be cast off, the steamer began to turn her paddles, and the ship gently moved from the wharf into the river amidst the deafening cheers of the people on the wharf. Just then four young men passengers who had no grief to express at parting from friends, jumped upon the deck of the upper cabin and sang in harmony and in very good voice the following song of the sea:

> A life on the ocean wave,
>   And a home on the rolling deep,
> Where the scattered waters rave
>   And the winds their revels keep.
> Like a bird in a cage I pine,
>   While on this stand-still shore;
> O, give me the pickly brine
>   And the good old ship once more.
> O, life on the ocean wave,
>   And a home on the rolling deep,
> Where the scattered waters rave
>   And the winds their revels keep.
>   CHORUS.
> And the winds, and the winds,
> And the winds their revels keep.

By the time the song was finished we were gliding down the Delaware river at an easy speed in tow of the steamer. At one o'clock the first dinner of the voyage was served. It consisted of roast beef, roast pork, boiled cabbage, sweet potatoes, Irish potatoes, stewed tomatoes and rice pudding. Thirty-one passengers sat at the table in the upper cabin, most of them strangers to one another.

The first one I heard speak was a German gentleman, who called out, "Steward, hoff you potato more?" At this strange kind of English the young Pennsylvanians burst into a roar of laughter, which served to break the ice of reserve, and a general conversation began to flow in a pleasant vein. I have enumerated the viands we had at our first dinner on the ship, and candor compels me to say that it was the last one we enjoyed of the kind during the voyage, for after that our fare consisted of salt beef, salt pork, beans, rice, codfish, mackerel, and potatoes while they lasted, which was about one month. Twice a week we had plum duff with raisins. The duff is composed of flour, lard, raisins, saloratus and water, with eggs mixed in when they can be had. When well mixed it is put into a canvas bag, wide at the top and very narrow at the bottom, boiled two hours and then turned out into a platter and served with wine sauce when it can be had, or else with vinegar, butter, sugar and water boiled well together and thickened with flour and flavored with nutmeg. On other days we had boiled rice, with sugar for dessert. The foregoing was the cabin fare on board the ship " Samson."

The steamboat towed the ship down the Delaware river as far as New Castle, where we came to anchor, and the steamer was ready to cast off; but just then there arose some trouble about the payment of the balance of the towage money. Capt. Blanchard came to me and said that if I would loan him what money I had, he would give me his note made payable in San Francisco, with six per cent. interest. I thought of the adage, "A bird in the hand is worth two in the bush," therefore I kept my money. The captain made a raise of the money from some of the other passengers and settled with the steamboatman and she was cast off and returned to Philadelphia. This was about three o'clock and the crew were turned to, to clear up the ship and make ready to start down the Delaware Bay.

Some of the passengers asked of the chief mate permission to take one of the quarter boats so as to go ashore. The mate said that he was willing, providing there were enough men among the passengers to manage the boat. This was easily done, and we rowed ashore and landed in New Castle. We found this to be a quiet, old fashioned town in the State of Delaware, and as we learned it was governed by old fashioned laws. We visited the courthouse and the jail, in the yard of which we were shown the pillory and the whipping post, where petty thieves and other criminals of low degree were triced up and flogged in the style of old colonial days. And it is claimed that the State of Delaware has a smaller percentage of criminals, according to population, than any other State in the Union.

That flogging is very efficacious in preventing crime has

been proven in many countries. At one time, when I was in Havana, Cuba, a negro slave, who had stolen a box of candles from a lot that was being discharged from the vessel that I belonged to, and taken in the very act, was at once brought before the magistrate. This was about nine o'clock in the morning. At ten o'clock I saw the same Negro being led by the *alguazil* or the constable and stood on the corner of the street, where the officer administered twelve lashes on the bare back with a blacksnake whip—the sentence being forty-eight lashes to be administered on the corners of four different streets facing the harbor. Our mate said to the clerk that was taking account of our cargo that it looked barbarous. The clerk said he knew it did, but if they did not practice such summary and vigorous measures that they would have to build more prisons than they had warehouses. "For," said he; "if we send a negro to jail he considers it a boon, because he obtains exemption from labor; for he is only taken out in the morning to sweep the streets and is allowed to pass the balance of the day in idleness, which all of his kind esteem a blessing." And it seems that the same disposition is manifested by idle and dissolute persons all over the world—they abhor work, but they dread a flogging.

We sauntered around the town until near dark and then we entered a large store, where they supplied the country people with a great variety of goods, besides edibles and drinkables, including an abundant supply of old Pennsylvania rye whisky, stored in the spacious cellar. The members of our party had begun to "wet their whistles" as soon as we got ashore, and when we went into this store the most of them bought one or two gallon demijohns full of old rye, wherewith to comfort themselves during the long voyage. The mugs of whisky in the meantime flew around pretty lively, and stories were told until it was time for us to return to the ship.

In our party was a retired ship captain, who had been enraptured by the stories of the gold discoveries in California and had determined to go out there with a stock of such goods as he thought he could sell. He had placed a large shipment on board the ship, such as tents, cooking utensils, blankets, and so forth. He was a broad faced, good natured looking man, and looked the very impersonation of good living. As Shakespeare has it,

"In fair, round belly, with good capon lined."

He was very jovial and very entertaining in his conversation. As he was well acquainted with the pilot who was to take the ship out to sea, he had obtained his permission to take along his seventeen year old son as far as Cape Henlopen, where the pilot boat would take off the pilot, and the captain's son would return to Philadelphia on board the first vessel that the pilot would take charge of to return.

We went to the boat landing and started for the ship. Everyone was jolly and hilarious, singing and laughing until we arrived alongside the ship. We secured the boat to the ship and began to climb the side ladder to go on board, when, unfortunately, one young man named Clayborn took hold of the manropes to climb up, but lost his grip and down he tumbled into the river between the ship and the boat. The potency of "old rye" had been too much for his nerves. We got him back into the boat after some confusion; a watch tackle was rigged and he was hoisted aboard the ship in a boatswain's chair, none the worse for the baptism which he had undergone. The mate ordered the quarterboat to be hoisted out of the water; the anchor watch was set and the crew went below. The passengers, one by one, turned into their berths to enjoy the first night's rest on board the ship.

As I said before, I had chosen my berth just abaft the pantry, and therefore not far from the front entrance to the cabin. As I laid in my berth I heard two men disputing on deck about the respective merits of General Scott and General Taylor, both of whom had been in command in Mexico. Brigadier General Taylor was first in command there and achieved very great victories, but he was supplanted by Major General Scott, who was his superior officer. There is no better way to describe the difference in the two men than by the soubriquet that was applied to each. General

Taylor was called "Old Rough and Ready," while General Scott was called "Old Fuss and Feathers." That tells the whole story. One fought off hand. The other was forever getting ready to fight.

TRAGEDY ON SHIPBOARD.

One of the passengers who was disputing with Capt. Brainard claimed to have been in Mexico with General Scott, and extolled his General. "What did he do?" asked the captain. "He took a 'hasty plate of soup,' didn't he?" "He commanded and I fought," said the volunteer. "You fought, did you? What did you fight—the commissary?" "I was in many battles," said the volunteer. "Oh, yes; in the canteen, I suppose," said the captain. "Look here, my brave soldier, while your friend General Scott can dispatch a 'hasty plate of soup,' my friend General Taylor can dispatch the enemy—horse, foot and dragoons."

After this sally there was silence for a spell. Then they began again in a maudlin way. All at once Capt. Brainard cried out, "You have cut me! you have cut me! Help! help!" I jumped out of my berth and ran out on deck, where I found Capt. Brainard lying across the top of the booby hatch with the blood flowing from his throat, while the other man stood coolly by silently looking on. I ran back into the cabin and gave the alarm. All the passengers arose from their berths, the captain was called from the lower cabin, and the wounded captain was taken into the cabin and laid upon the table. An examination showed that his throat was cut from ear to ear. The captain ordered the quarter boat lowered and manned. The mate was ordered to go ashore at once and get the sheriff and the doctor. The captain requested me to go with the mate, which I did. We went ashore while Doctor Doriot, one of the passengers, put bandages around the neck of the wounded man.

When we arrived ashore it was twelve o'clock. As we walked up the broad street we saw a light in one house only. We went up to it and found that it was the hotel. The mate told the man in attendance what had occurred on board of our ship, and said that he wanted to get the sheriff and a doctor. The man directed us, and the mate told me to go for the doctor while he went for the sheriff, and we would meet at the boat at the landing. I went, accompanied by one of the sailors, and aroused the doctor, told him what had taken place, and begged his attendance. He at once prepared himself, took his satchel, and accompanied us to the boat. When we arrived at the landing we found the mate, the sheriff and his deputy already there. We shoved off at once and hurried to the ship.

When the doctor took the bandages off the patient's neck and examined him, he declared that it was a most miraculous escape from instant death. He said if the wound had been inflicted upon any other person then present—and he looked around him—it would have severed his jugular vein and he would have at once bled to death. He then opened his satchel, took out from it his paraphernalia and sewed up and dressed the wound. He ordered the patient to be taken ashore at once.

A tackle was rigged and an arm-chair was slung, and the wounded man was gently lowered into the boat and stretched out in the stern sheets. In this way he was taken ashore, and, attended by the doctor, carried to the hotel. The other quarter boat was now lowered into the water and the sheriff and his deputy took the culprit in charge and were rowed ashore.

The pilot went ashore with his wounded friend and saw that he was comfortably placed in bed in the hotel, and left him in charge of the doctor. The pilot persuaded Capt. Brainard to allow his son to take his place on board the ship and take charge of his papers, and when the pilot returned from Cape Henlopen he would bring back the father's trunks with the exception of such articles of wearing apparel as the son could use on the voyage out. All this being arranged satisfactorily the pilot returned to the ship and explained to Capt. Blanchard what had been done, and he seemed to acquiesce. The mate told the captain that the sheriff had notified him to come on shore in the morning with all those persons that were cognizant of what had taken place on board the ship. The pilot interposed, and advised the captain that, it being three o'clock in the morning and the wind having sprung up light in the northwest, that the best thing to be done was to up anchor and get immediately under way, before any legal papers could be served on the people on board. The reasoning of the pilot was so cogent that he consented that the pilot should at once get the ship under way and proceed down the bay.

When the mate explained to the passengers the threatened legal detention, every one, even the Frenchmen, took right hold and helped to heave up the anchor, and pulled and hauled until the ship was under way and scooting down the bay under a freshening breeze.

By six o'clock in the morning we were quite a distance down the bay. The wind being fair, the mate ordered the topmast studdingsails to be bent and sent out. Next the topgallant studdingsails were set, and the ship was making eight knots an hour.

During the forenoon every time that we saw a fast sailing schooner overtaking us, we thought she had the sheriff on board to intercept us. Our fears were groundless, as many fast sailers passed us without taking any notice of us. By dinner time the passengers who had been apprehensive of being detained regained their equanimity and ate their dinner with a relish. The northwester was now growing strong. The studdingsails were taken in, and the white caps on the bay began to give us a premonition of what we might expect when we got outside. By five P. M. we were abreast of Cape Henlopen breakwater, heading for sea. At half-past five the pilot boat came up under our starboard quarter and launched her dingey.

The captain took charge of the ship and ordered the courses to be hauled up and brought the ship to the wind. The mainyards were hove back and the little dingey bobbed up under our lee. The captain ordered the steward to toss a big chunk of beef into the dingey. The captain and the pilot descended into the lower cabin, presumably to take an observation through the bottom of a glass. They returned on deck wiping the moisture from their lips. The pilot spoke a few words to the son of Capt. Brainard, shook hands with the captain, wished him a safe and pleasant voyage, and descended to the dingey, shoved off, and was quickly rowed to the pilot boat.

As soon as the pilot left the captain ordered the helm to be put hard up, and the mainyards to be swung round. The ship was soon on her course and all sails were set. It was now 6:30 P. M. and we were now on the broad Atlantic, with the prospect of sailing many thousands of miles, and passing through many vicissitudes before we could set our feet on "terra firma" again.

The captain took his departure from Cape Henlopen, Lat. 38° 47' N., Long. 75° 05' W., distance twelve miles, bearing west by north. This was all noted down for the reason that if the sun should be obscured the following day the position of the ship could be ascertained by the distance run and the course that was steered. This is called dead-reckoning. The anchor chains were now unshackled and the plugs driven into the hawse holes. The headboards were taken in and the decks were cleared up. The breeze was freshening. The three royals were taken in and the mainsail was hauled up and furled. Our course was south-east, and the sea began to rise, making the ship roll just as easy as an old fashioned cradle.

At half-past seven o'clock the mate called all the sailors to the waist of the ship and ranged them in line so as to choose the watches. The first mate chose the first man, and that happened to be the man that was at that moment at the wheel. The second mate, whose name was Bryson, chose the second man, so alternating until the twelve men were selected—six men in each watch—the first mate having the larboard watch and the second mate the starboard, or what is called the captain's watch. At eight bells, that was eight o'clock, the log was thrown (which is a measuring line divided into knots which mark a nautical mile to each knot), and it marked nine knots—or nine nautical miles per hour. The ship was now at her best speed, as she had a fair wind, and besides, all that she wanted. The second mate had the first watch of four hours duration, terminating at twelve o'clock, midnight; or, as it is called at sea, eight bells.

Now commenced the sea mode of marking time. At half-past eight o'clock the man at the wheel struck one stroke on a small bell that was suspended upon a brass bell gallows, over the binnacle, where the compass is placed to guide the helmsman to steer the ship on her course. When the small bell sounded the stroke one, the man forward on the lookout ran to a much larger or what is called the ship's bell and responded by striking one stroke. So it continued to strike at the expiration of every half hour until the end of the watch, or twelve o'clock, which was eight bells. Then the other watch was called on deck and the watch that had already served four hours went below to sleep four hours. At half-past twelve the bell was struck one stroke, as at half-past eight, and each half hour was added one stroke until the end of the watch of four hours. In order to alternate the watches so that one watch shall not serve at the same period every night and day, one four-hour watch, that from 4 P. M. to 8 P. M., is divided into two watches, called the dog watches. This causes the watch that serves from 8 P. M. till 12, midnight, one night, to serve from 12, midnight, until 4 A. M. the next morning, so alternating unceasingly to the end of the voyage.

The first night at sea was a novelty to many of the passengers on board, and as the wind was fair northwest, the sky clear, and the air mild, many of them stayed up late. Mr. Bryson, the second mate, who had charge of the watch, told me that he was a native Philadelphian and had sailed for many years in Cope's line of Liverpool packets. He said he was bound now to make one grand stroke for a fortune in the mines of California, and return home and buy a little farm in Chester County and settle down with his family, "under his own vine and fig tree, with none to molest or make him afraid."

The ship was steering about southeast and going along with an easy, rolling motion, that made newcomers think that going to sea was not such a hardship after all. About ten o'clock, or four bells, I turned in; and to me it was a novel experience, for never had I been on board of a ship before, since I ceased to be a cabin boy, without having a watch to stand some time during the night.

I arose at five o'clock, or two bells, the next morning, and saw that the wind had moderated. The royals were set and the starboard watch were engaged in getting up the lower studding sails out of the booby hatch. By seven bells all the studding sails had been set alow and aloft. The two immense lower studding sails, with long, swinging booms, made the ship look like some gigantic bird, skimming the water with its great wings spread. At eight o'clock, when the steward rang the bell to summon the passengers to breakfast, I went to the table and found there were six of us only. The balance of them were either looking over the side or lying helplessly in their berths. The rest of us had to eat, and we did eat. We had fried ham, boiled hominy, hot biscuit and coffee.

All this day the crew were kept busy making everything snug on deck—lashing spars, water casks, barrels of beef, pork and crates of potatoes and onions. The ship was now rolling before the wind like an old fashioned seventy-four gun ship. Every few minutes the lower stun' sail booms would swoop into the water, first on one side, then on the other, with force enough to almost wrench them from their sockets in the deck stanchions.

At twelve meridian the captain, who had been observing the sun with his sextant, sung out, "Twelve o'clock!" at which the man at the wheel struck eight bells, and the bell abaft the foremast was struck responsive; the mate corrected the marine clock in the binnacle to correspond to the change in longitude.

When the dinner bell rang at one o'clock, the same persons appeared as at breakfast. They, being old shellbacks, were not affected by the motion of the ship. The dinner consisted of salt beef, salt pork, cabbage, potatoes, and plum duff with wine sauce. There we sat and enjoyed our dinner, while the poor fellows that were lying in their berths wished that they had gone to California by ox team or stayed at home in comfort. But we knew that their discomfort was only temporary and that in a day or two they would be able to eat their allowance with a better relish than they ever did before.

It must be borne in mind that a man who started for California in those days had to be a man of substance, with sufficient means to support his family during his absence and have enough besides to pay his own expenses to reach the land of gold. Therefore, it may be safely said that a finer, more enterprising or determined body of men never collected before, than those that came to California from the year 1849 to 1852.

Our fellow passengers were unnerved and weakened by the terrible seasickness, but when they recovered from it and their natural buoyant ambition reasserted itself, they showed themselves to be men fit to found a State on the Pacific Slope.

The fair wind continued for two days, after which it moderated to a four knot breeze and the sky became overclouded. We were now approaching the Gulf Stream, and the captain ordered one of the men to draw a bucket of water from over the ship's side, wherein he immersed the thermometer, to ascertain the temperature of the ocean.

The Gulf Stream is a subaqueous stream of water that commences to flow in the Gulf of Mexico, thence into the Straits of Florida between the Florida Coast and the Island of Cuba and the Bahama Islands. Its course is to the northeast and its speed, between the Capes of Florida and the

Double-headed Shot Keys is often as much as six miles per hour. It pours into the Atlantic Ocean, continuing its course within a distance of from two hundred to as near as forty miles from the coast off Cape Hatteras, until it loses itself beyond the Labrador Coast in the vicinity of the Banks of New Foundland. The temperature is from ten to fifteen degrees warmer than the water on each side of it. In the winter time vessels that approach the Gulf Stream from the frozen coast of New England can discern it by the dense vapor that hangs over it, reminding them of a huge cauldron of boiling water emitting volumes of steam. The Gulf Stream is much more liable to storms than the Atlantic Ocean is on either side of it.

We were now getting into the gulf stream and the captain was apprehensive of the approach of the line gale, so called because the sun crosses the equator to the south about the twenty-second of September, and it is always followed by a gale of wind, more or less severe, within a month thereafter.

In the month of October, 1843, was the most terrific and disastrous gale of any known up to that time on the coast of New England. Cape Cod and Cape Ann alone lost more than forty vessels that had been engaged in fishing and coasting. The devastating effects of the gale reached as far south as the Savannah river. Therefore, knowing all this, the captain was very careful for the safety of the ship.

At 8 P. M., the wind being baffling and the sky obscured by heavy clouds, the captain ordered the second mate, who had the first watch that night, to call him if there was the least change in the weather. The barometer was falling, which was a sure indication of an approaching change in the weather and a probable storm. At four bells the wind was like a faint breath and the sails were lazily flapping against the masts with every undulation of the ship. At six bells the second mate watched the barometer, which hung in the upper cabin, and found that the mercury was falling apace. The indications were so threatening that the second mate went into the lower cabin and called Capt. Blanchard. He soon came on deck with his English pea-jacket and his sou'-wester on and trumpet in hand. He scanned the weather horizon for a minute and then told the second mate to call all hands.

I was standing on the quarter deck when the captain came up, and when I saw his fine, manly form and his commanding appearance, it inspired me with a confidence in his ability as a master of a ship. But, I thought, what a pity it was that so fine and dignified a body should contain so small and narrow soul. The watch soon tumbled up and in the meantime the captain had ordered the royals and topgallant sails to be furled. Next the courses were hauled up and furled, the fore and main spencers were brailed up, and the flying jib was stowed. It now began to spit rain, and was as dark as a nigger's pocket.

The second mate reported to the captain that the barometer stood 29.05. Still there was no wind. The fore and mizzentopsails were clewed down and furled. Then the maintopsail was close reefed and the jib was hauled down and stowed. Now the ship was under snug sail, close reefed maintopsail, forestaysail and the spanker, still there was no wind, but there were portentious signs of impending trouble.

About eight bells there was a sound in the air like the escaping of suppressed steam, sounding like "sizzz, sizzz." The sound grew louder and louder and nearer. The sea began to display phosphorescent glittering particles as though it was in a blaze. The sky was as black as a pall. All at once the gale struck the ship and threw her nearly on her beam ends. I never received such a shock in all my experience. The maintopsail, although nearly new and close reefed, was blown out of the boltropes as if it had been tissue paper. The spanker followed the topsail, while the forestaysail held its own. The captain ordered the helm to be put hard up, and ordered an additional man to the wheel. The ship obeyed the helm promptly and began to pay off and was soon before the wind. The forestaysail was now taken in and the ship was scudding under bare poles before the terrible hurricane. At the first blast of the gale the sea was comparatively smooth, but in a short time the big combers began to lift near the stern. An hour after the gale struck the ship the seas were running mountains high. We were running before a terrific southeaster, and the ship creaked and groaned in every joint and it seemed as if she could not hold together. Great combers arose near our stern, as if they were about to engulf us, but each time the ship would shoot ahead and escape. The captain ordered that life lines be placed around the waists of the two men at the helm, and that the ends be well secured. The huge waves, with crested heads, would seem like living sea monsters looking at us, fifty feet over our heads, as though they would overwhelm and engulf us at once. The ship behaved beautifully and proved herself a fine seaboat, and rose and fell in harmony with each passing wave as it swept past us. All at once an ugly towering wave approached the ship from astern. It came with overwhelming force. The captain sung out, "Look out!" and the sea came over the stern and pooped the ship. It swept everything before it. The two men at the helm were carried from their post as if they had been two wisps of straw, but the precautionary measures taken by the captain saved them, and the life lines enabled them to save themselves from injury. The lower cabin skylight was wrenched from its fastenings and the cabin was drenched with water. The starboard quarter boat was lifted from its fastenings and wedged between the bulwark and the upper cabin. The ship was waterlogged, and everything that was not well secured on the main deck was floating around, thereby endangering the lives of the men, who were hanging on to anything that was solid enough to hold on by. The upper cabin was full of water up to the first tier of berths. The steward and the cook, who had their room abaft the galley, were nearly carried overboard, but were saved by the brawny arms of the second mate, Mr. Bryson. The ship had nearly lost her steerageway. The captain and mate were the first to jump to the helm, and for five minutes it seemed as if it was all up with us. After that the ship began to free herself and obeyed her helm.

The decks were being freed from the water that was swashing about, and we began to breathe easier.

Daylight now began to appear, and the captain ordered the mate to get out a new maintopsail out of the sailroom and have it bent. All hands were set to work, and after long continued labor and much risk, it was bent. It was at once close reefed and set. Now came the most dangerous performance that a ship can be subjected to when she has been running before the wind in a gale; that is, to bring her up to the wind without swamping her. The captain ordered all hands to man the braces, and watched his opportunity—for in the severest gale there are periods when the waves don't break so hard, for a short spell, as they do in its most furious moments. The watched for chance came. "Port your helm four spokes," said the captain. "Aye, aye, sir!" was answered by the man at the wheel. "Ease away on your starboard braces and haul in on your lee ones." It was done. The ship came up gently—she came up to the trough of the sea. Now was our greatest danger. "Hard down your helm! Slack away on your weather braces and haul in sharp on your lee ones." The ship came up sharply, and just then a sea struck her amidships and broke over the starboard side and partially filled the decks, but the ship continued to come up to the wind until she lay close to the wind, and was lying to with an easy motion.

The captain now ordered the steward to go down into the run of the ship and draw a bucket of New England rum and bring it on deck. The rum was brought up, and also a pitcher and two tumblers, and placed near the capstan. The captain told the mate to treat the men. Mr. Bryson, the second mate, sang out: "Lay aft here, all hands, and splice the main brace!" "Aye, aye, sir!" responded the men in one voice, as they hurried aft to the capstan. Then Mr. Bryson filled the pitcher from the bucket of rum and served each man with a generous nip in the tumbler. When all the sailors had been served, then came his turn to serve himself and the good-hearted Mr. Bryson took the traditional second mate's nip, four fingers and a thumb; or, more plainly speaking, the biggest of the two tumblers, brimful, as the motion of the ship allowed. After this hearty swig he took a long breath, smacked his lips, and said: "I wish my mother had fed me with just such porridge as that."

It was soon discovered that the ship being trimmed too much by the stern she payed off too much and shipped some water. The captain then ordered the storm trysail to be brought up and bent; as soon as this aftersail was put on the ship, although it was a very small sail made of extra heavy canvas, it brought the ship up to the wind, and she rode like a duck on the water, for the storm trysail, at the mizzen, kept her nose well up to the wind and she rode safely. The barometer had now fallen to 29°, and the gale continued unabated, and the wind veered from east southeast to south southeast.

This terrible storm reminded me of the words of Holy Writ: "Thou breakest the ships of Tarshish with an east wind"—(48th Psalms, 7th verse). Thus showing clearly that even in the day of King David the east wind was greatly dreaded.

Now that everything had been made as snug as possible under the very trying circumstances, the men whose watch was below were allowed to go to their four hours rest, which they sadly needed; while the watch on deck had only to stand by the helm, which was kept hard down and lashed there, while one man kept a look-out ahead. These men, when passing about the decks, were obliged to hold on to the life-lines that had been stretched fore and aft along the bulwarks. Thus the ship continued for two days.

During this time we had not seen the sun for more than two minutes at a time, therefore we were unable to obtain an observation; for that reason the captain had to trust to his dead-reckoning in order to ascertain the position of the ship.

On the third night, about nine o'clock, when darkness of the densest kind prevailed and the wind was whistling through the rigging and producing sounds like a mournful requiem, a phenomenon appeared which struck fear into the stoutest heart. This was the appearance of three lightning balls or corposants—one on the main truck, and one each on the ends of the maint'gallant yard. This, it was thought, portended some dreadful catastrophe. It caused every one that saw it to feel very uneasy. Although I had seen the like before I still was now very seriously impressed by this awful sign in the heavens, under such conditions, with wind roaring, the great waves mountain high and foaming and breaking. I derived comfort from the poetic lines of Thomas Dibden: "There is a sweet little Cherub who sits up aloft that looks out for the life of poor Jack." These words gave me much comfort and did much to allay my apprehensions.

By 10 P. M. the gale began to abate. It would blow violently for ten to fifteen minutes and then gradually subside. By 11 o'clock P. M. there was a change taking place in the weather. It had been dark up to that time, but it became so dark now that a man could not see his hand before him. The chief mate went and called the captain, who came on deck at once. As the ship was under the shortest possible sail, nothing more could be done in that direction. We waited for events. The three fiery balls had vanished, and the wind had lulled to a mere breeze. The ship was now rolling and pitching in obedience to the motion of the tumbling waves. Suddenly, without premonition, there was a blinding flash of lightning that illuminated the space around and showed every part of the ship and masts and rigging as clearly as if it had been high noon on a clear day. Then followed a noise so tremendous that it was indescribable. Just imagine that one thousand steam railroad engines, coming from opposite directions and meeting on a bridge that spans a mountain over a chasm hundreds of feet in depth, and in the very center of it coming in contact and crashing in one fell swoop and falling to the very bottom of the abyss, and the same instant exploding the boilers of every one of them. This would be dreadful, but it would bear but a faint comparison to the clap of thunder which followed the lightning's flash. Every man on the deck was thrown down by the dreadful shock. The ship trembled like an aspen leaf, and we all thought that the thunderbolt had struck her, but, thanks to a kind Providence, she was spared. This was followed by a stillness that was painful to experience. Every man on board the ship jumped out of his berth and waited in fear and trembling for what would come next. We soon felt large drops of rain falling; it came faster and more of it, until it seemed as if the very floodgates of heaven had been entirely opened. It poured in such volume that the scuppers could not free the deck and the portholes had to be opened. The men had to hold on to life lines while they were wading about the deck, and whatever small articles that were not secured floated out to sea through the portholes. The sea, which had been so rough, was actually beaten down by the force of the rain to the smoothness of a millpond.

In about half an hour the rain began to slack. There were rifts in the clouds that allowed us to get a glimpse of the clear blue sky. Soon the rain ceased altogether and the beautiful blue vault of heaven, with its myriad of stars, was again in full view, while the clouds were rolling to the south and southeast. A breeze sprung up from the nor'west and the captain ordered the fore and mizzentopsails set, and the reefs to be shaken out of the maintopsail. The courses were next loosed and dropped, and one after another every sail was set to the favoring breeze. Daylight was now coming on apace and brought to my mind the beautiful hymn:

"The light of day is breaking,
The darkness disappears."

All hands were now busy making sail, as the weather was now promising in its signs. The barometer had risen to 30, and still rising. Soon the rays in the eastern horizon gave us premonition of the coming of the beautiful orb of day, the sun. It soon arose from its ocean bed in all its glorious effulgence, giving promise of a clear day and pleasant weather. Our hearts now turned to God in silent thankfulness for his mercy and loving kindness in having thus spared us from a terrible fate.

"The spacious firmanent on high,
With all the blue ethereal sky,
And spangled heaven's shining frame,
Their great original proclaim.
The unwearied sun from day to day,
Does his creator's powers display,
And publishes to every land,
The work of an almighty hand."

At 8 A. M. the mate came on deck with his sextant and observed the altitude of the sun, while the captain marked the time by the chronometer in the cabin. By this process the navigator can ascertain the distance, east or west, from Greenwich, which is the initial point for longitude in all the English and American charts.

At 12 meridian, when the sun had reached its zenith, the captain and the mate having noted its altitude in degrees by sextant, figured out the latitude, thereby ascertaining the exact position of the ship upon the broad ocean, thereby proving the advantages of the noble science of navigation. During the day the deck and lower rigging were covered with a miscellaneous collection of sailors' and passengers' clothing which had been hung up to dry, reminding me of the second-hand clothing stores on Chatham street, in New York. Every face on board the ship wore a smiling look. The terrible experience which we had passed through had produced a softening influence on all of us. On this day the cook exerted himself and prepared a sea pie for our dinner. A sea pie consists of onions fried brown, lean pork, cut in small pieces, potatoes cut in quarters, and then all simmered together; then make dough enough to cover the sides of the baking pan, and after the sides are covered, put in the filling of stew, season with tomato ketchup and pepper, sprinkle in a little dry flour to thicken it, and cover the pan with a thick crust and put it in the oven for two hours. In the absence of chicken or fresh beef this is a very palatable dish. Besides the pie we had a large plum-duff. The dinner was eaten with thankful hearts which gave it relish, it being the first regular cooked dinner in four days. The weather had now settled down pleasant with a steady six knot breeze. We now discovered a new source of worriment and anxiety. The late gale had so strained the ship that she had began to leak quite seriously. Pumping the usual time of fifteen minutes we found that the water was not out of the ship, so the second mate took the sounding rod and shoved it down into the pumpwell. When he drew out the rod he measured, and found that at least fourteen inches of water remained in the ship. The ship had two very fine metallic pumps which the captain said had been placed in her on the last voyage he made to Liverpool. They were worked by a rotary crank attached to which was a very heavy flywheel, and the two pumps threw water quite equal in volume to a fire engine. With this double geared apparatus the crew, with the aid of the passengers, freed the ship of the water in the space of two hours. When the pumps began to suck our fears were relieved, for it proved to us that the leak was not beyond our control.

The captain now ordered the mates to have the ship pumped out every two hours instead of every four hours as heretofore. This increased leak of course augmented the labor of the crew very much and thereby created a certain measure of discontent among them, and more particularly as their food was inferior in quality, and not very well prepared at that, as the captain never approached the galley or seemed to care as to how his sailors fared. The cook took advantage of the indifference of the captain about the welfare of the sailors and served out their food in a happy-go-lucky kind of manner, that proved the truth of the old adage, " like master like man," and the sailors were the sufferers. Salt meat, not soaked and but half cooked, beans as hard as bullets, and the duff as heavy as lead. As I was a sailor myself I took notice of all this.

We were now in latitude 31 07 N., and longitude 52 15 W. The gale of the past week had driven us back over the greatest part of our distance previously gained; but now we had settled, clear weather and a fair wind. The passengers now cast about for something to do in order that the time might pass by pleasantly. Reading and talking becomes irksome after a time; therefore a class was formed to learn the French language. Mon. Bayard, a learned French gentleman, was selected to be the teacher, but we soon found out that in order to teach us the French language he would be obliged to first learn the English language. In order to overcome this difficulty we appealed to Dr. Doriot, a gentleman who was born in Philadelphia of French parents, and therefore was thoroughly conversant with the French language as well as his native English. The doctor showed no disposition to aid us. He preferred to read French novels and smoke cigars at his ease. For this reason we made but sorry progress with our French lessons.

Capt. Blanchard was a man that boasted a great deal about what he used to do when he was mate in the "Black Ball" line of packets that ran between New York and Liverpool. That, as a mate of a ship, he had never been in a vessel where there was an afternoon watch below allowed, and as master of a ship he had never allowed it nor would he allow it on this voyage only at such times as when the ship would be put under double reefed topsails. At other times, all hands should be on deck from 1 P. M. till 5 P. M., at which time the men could take their supper. He instructed his two mates to enforce this rule—under this rule all hands had to work on the rigging, or making chafing mats or mending the sails, during the afternoons. His boast was that when he was mate of the ship "Roscius," of the "Black Ball" line, that the shipping master would put a crew on board who would give it out on board that they were determined to carry everything before them with a high hand; but they would find out, to their sorrow, before the ship arrived in Liverpool, that they had reckoned without their host. "For," said he, "my rule with sailors was a word and a blow, and the blow came first. I was at one time mate with Capt. Jabez Percival, an old Cape Cod man, on the ship 'Lady Siddons.' And he used to say to me, 'Walk into the scoundrels, Mr. Blanchard, and I'll back you up, sir. Give it to 'em, right and left, and keep 'em on a jump. I'll tell you what, Mr. Blanchard, there was an old Grand Bank fishing captain in my town named Capt. Dean Linnell, and he was noted for bringing home every fall a larger catch of codfish than any other Grand Banker that cleared out of the Barnstable custom house. His motto was: "I'll keep no more cats than what will catch mice." And every man that ships aboard my schooner is given to understand that his fishing line must be kept over the side every day, excepting Sundays, or when the weather will not permit it. And from the strict adherence to this practice comes my success.' Then," said the captain, "keep all hands on deck, Mr. Cranston, all afternoons when the weather will permit." The leak was not increasing but it was bad enough to keep the watch pumping for half an hour in every two hours; this, added to their regular duties, made it quite severe on the crew.

It was the fifteenth day out, in the forenoon, while I was sitting on a water cask over the main hatch, that Capt. Blanchard came to where I sat and saluted me in a most cordial manner. "Well," said he, "What are you reading so earnestly?" "I am reading the life of Benjamin Franklin." "Well, that is an instructive book; but it seems to me that time must hang very heavy on your hands." "No, sir; I like to read instructive books, and Franklin lays down some excellent maxims for young men, to guide them in life." He then proceeded: "What do you think of the gale that we have passed through?" "I think, sir, that it was the most severe that I ever have experienced." "Is that so?" "Yes, sir." "While I admit that it was a pretty severe spell of bad weather, I'll tell you it wasn't a circumstance to the one I was in when I was mate of the 'Shakspeare,' in the 'Black Ball' line, with Capt. Nye in command—and a better man never trod a ship's deck. We left New York for Liverpool on the thirtieth day of November. As we passed out by Sandy Hook the wind was west nor'west and a stiff breeze. The weather was clear and a high barometer. We put every inch of canvas on the ship, and she felt it. It sent her a-kiting through the water. We came up with a number of coasters and we went by them as if they were lying at anchor. We carried the breeze varying from west nor'west to west southwest, until we were over the banks of New Foundland, and we had a fine prospect for a quick passage. The crew, as is usual in the Liverpool trade, were a hard set. But I had a splendid after guard. The second mate, Simpson by name, was a regular Hercules in size, and was as spry as a cat. When I first got acquainted with him he was taking a little recreation on shore, and to pay expenses had hired a room in Maiden Lane and was giving lessons in boxing. I was introduced to him by a friend who was mate of the ship 'Prince Albert,' and visited his place on such evenings as I could spare from my other engagements while in port. I considered myself no chicken in handling my flippers at that time, and I put on the boxing gloves with him, after paying one dollar, which was his price for each lesson of half an hour's duration. The first evening of the lesson he let me have everything my own way. I tapped him on his bread-basket, tickled him in the ribs, punched him on the nose, and gave him a whack on the chin. Well, sir, I was fairly beside myself with delight. I never had such a high opinion of my skill before that evening, after my bout with Simpson. He congratulated me for my skill and quickness, while several of the spectators, who had been looking on, shook hands with me, and said I was a trump. Simpson had a small bar fitted up at the further end of the room, which was attended to by an old shipmate of his. I asked all hands up to smile; and all hands did smile. That took another two dollars, but I didn't mind the expense, for I felt grand. Simpson asked me when would I call upon him again? I replied that it would be impossible to come the next evening as I had an engagement, but on the evening following I would come, sure. So I left him, feeling myself to be equal to Tom Hyer, the celebrated pugilist of New York.

"The second evening after that I went to Simpson's boxing school, paid my dollar, put on the boxing gloves to take my half hour lesson. He had a larger number of scholars than he had when I was there the first time. He put on his gloves and we stood facing each other. I didn't like his looks. He looked wicked around the eyes. I began to lose confidence in myself; but I stood up to him, as I knew that he would not hit very hard. However, he sung out to me, 'Look out.' When bang! went his right on my chin. Next his left caromed on my stomach. Then he swiped me all round. In fact, I found Simpson to be a complete thrashing machine. In fifteen minutes I had all the boxing lesson that I wanted for that night. I took off the gloves, treated all hands, and bid them all good night. Well, sir, I felt mortified; I was completely cowed. I had the conceit thoroughly taken out of me. The truth was that whereas I had thought myself a pretty tough man to handle, Simpson had taught me that I was but a baby in the fighting line. I conceived a plan in my mind and proceeded to carry it out. On the next evening I called upon Simpson and proposed to him that he join the 'Shakspeare' on the next voyage if I could arrange the matter with Capt. Nye. He agreed to do so, providing that I could make a definite engagement with him before the ship sailed. I approached the subject with Capt. Nye by speaking of the second mate, whose name was Sears, and said to the captain that while Sears was an ambitious and industrious young man that he was not equal to handling a crew that was composed of such a hard lot as was generally found on board of a 'Black Ball' liner, and consequently it was my opinion that a man of more force of character and greater determination would secure far better service in working the ship. I then told him of a man that I knew who had been second mate of the packet ship 'Lady Washington,' but was now disengaged, and probably could be secured for the next voyage. I studiously refrained from mentioning anything about his pugilistic abilities, because it might have prejudiced the captain against him. For, while Capt. Nye never interfered with me in the management of the crew, he well knowing that they scarcely ever made more than one voyage in the same ship, still he was averse to having any trouble between his officers and his men if it could be avoided. Capt. Nye was somewhat religious in his predilections, so much so that he at one time bought a magnificent bible, and purple cushion to place it on, for the pulpit of the church in which he worshiped in his boyhood days, in his native town in Massachusetts. At another time he had a large bell cast in Troy, New York, which he sent to his native town to be placed in the belfry of the same church. Therefore, knowing his conservative disposition, I said nothing about Simpson's knocking down proclivities. When I pointed out the advantage that would accrue to the working of the ship he gave his consent for me to engage Simpson to come on board when the ship returned from Liverpool. Before we left I made the arrangement with Simpson to join the ship on the next voyage. At the time of which I am now speaking we had laid in the stream for two days waiting for a crew. Most of the sailors that sailed in the Liverpool packets during the summer months preferred to ship to go by the run to New Orleans or Mobile in the fall of the year and spend the winter in the south loading ships with cotton for Europe, and in the spring, when the season of business activity had ended, they would ship in cotton loaded ships for Liverpool or Havre, at $25.00 or $30.00 for the run. There they would enjoy themselves while the money lasted, and then make their way back to America. For this reason we had to take such men as the shipping master could pick up. In consequence we had as villainous a looking twenty men as I ever was shipmates with.

"During the first two days after we left Sandy Hook all hands were engaged securing everything about the decks and putting on the chafing gear. It had been my practice to have both watches on deck from 1 P. M. till 5 P. M., every day excepting Sunday or when stormy weather prevented it. Well, as I said before, Simpson was the second mate; Stevens the bos'n was an Irishman, and he was a terror to evildoers; then there was Chips the carpenter, and Olsen the sailmaker, everyone of 'em as true as steel, and could be depended on. Well, sir, on the third day out, at 1 o'clock in the afternoon, I told the bos'n to turn all hands to work.

He went forward to the forecastle, which was in the forward deck house, which was divided into galley in the after part and forecastle in the forward part, which had a door on each side. He called all hands to turn to work. But not a man stepped out on deck. He went the second time with the same result.

"I held a short consultation with the second mate, after which I called the carpenter and the sailmaker, who were located by themselves, and with bos'n just abaft the mainmast, and ordered them to join us, and we went forward in a body. I stood in the doorway of the forecastle and sung out: 'Come out of that, every one of you!' But not a man stirred. Then the leader spoke up and said: 'I have made many a winter passage from New York to Liverpool and this is the first time I was ever called upon to turn to work in my afternoon watch below, after everything was made snug and the chafing gear put on; and I will speak for myself and all my shipmates—we are not going to do it now. Either give us the afternoon watch below or you may sail the ship yourself.' No sooner had he spoken than I made a jump for him. As I grabbed him by his collar he let fly at me with his right fist. But I had been there before, and I warded off the blow, which he intended should be a sockdolager for me. I let go my grip on him, and fetched him a blow under his ear which felled him like an ox. At this Simpson sailed in, and the bos'n wasn't behind hand, while Chips and the sailmaker brought up the rear.

"Simpson maintained his reputation in splendid style. He would take a man by the nape of the neck and the slack of his breeches and would toss him out on deck the same as if he had been a feather pillow. After a half dozen of them had been thrown into the lee scuppers the balance of them didn't stand upon the order of their going but went out on deck at once. Every man went to work just as if nothing had happened, and I must say that a better set of men I never had under my control than what they proved themselves to be after that day.

"As I said, we had the prospect of a quick run to Cape

Clear until the fourteenth day, when the wind moderated and the weather showed signs of a change taking place. The clouds began to gather in the eastward. The wind had backed around to east nor'east and it was light and baffling. The barometer was falling, and all signs betokened the approach of a gale. The captain ordered that all the light sails be taken in and the topsails be double reefed. We kept her along under double reefed topsails and courses for a while. In the meantime the swell was coming from the nor'east, which presaged a blow from that quarter. I had the first watch on deck that night and the captain told me to call him if any change took place. About four bells the wind from the nor'east began to freshen and pipe up pretty lively. I called the captain, who came on deck at once. After five minutes he ordered the mainsail to be hauled up and furled. The jib was taken in and stowed. The foresail was hauled up and furled. The spanker was taken in and the ship was now under double reefed topsails, foretopmast staysail, and fore and main spencers. Finally, the ship was put under close reefed maintopsail, foretopmast staysail, and the storm trysail at the mizzen. The wind kept increasing, and the barometer fell to 29 inches—a sure sign of a heavy blow. A drizzling rain began to fall, and finally we had to take everything but the close reefed maintopsail, mizzen storm trysail, and foretopmast staysail. At seven bells the gale had so much increased that we had to take in everything and heave the ship to under close reefed maintopsail.

"I went below at 1 A. M. and turned into my berth, having taken off my peajacket and boots. I was in a light sleep when I was startled by a crashing and thundering sound that shook the ship like a reed. I rushed upon deck and everything was in the utmost confusion. The ship was taking aboard water, over the lee bulwarks, by the ton, while the three topgallantmasts—which had been carried away clear down to the caps—were dangling, held by the rigging, and pounding the ship, on the lee side, at every plunge she made. The captain ordered the wreck of spars to be cut and cleared away, as nothing could be saved from them; and then we proceeded to make everything safe. But we had not seen it all yet, for the ship dipped her bow into a heavy sea which filled the decks with water, and when she raised, we found that the jib-boom and the flying jib-boom had both been carried away, and were pounding the ship abreast of the lee forerigging. Then all hands turned to and made every effort to save some of the paraphernalia, but without avail, as the seas were making a clean breach over the ship, making it impossible to work, so that everything had to be cut away and clear from the ship. The ship now looked very dilapidated. But after the wreck of the spars and rigging were cleared away she laid close to the wind and rode the waves with dry decks. Well, we were hove-to for five successive days, and as the wind and current had taken us as far south as 40 degrees of latitude we were nearly as far south as the Azores Islands.

"On the sixth day after the gale came on the weather began to improve, the wind moderated and all hands turned to work to repair damages that had been caused by the gale. The wind veered around to the southward and we shaped our course for Saint George's Channel. The carpenter was set to work to get out the three new to'gallant masts and a jib-boom. We had rough spars enough, also had some already prepared to answer for to'gallant yards. Simpson, who could handle a drawing knife or a spoke shave as deftly as a carpenter, turned in to help Chips while I took charge of the refitting of the rigging. We got out the maintopgallantmast first, sent it up and fitted the yards and sails. Then followed the jib-boom and all the other spars in rapid succession until by the time we entered Saint George's Channel everything aloft was 'shipshape and Bristol fashion.'

"As we approached the Mersey the pilot came on board. He told the captain that the consignees of the cargo had become apprehensive that the ship would never arrive in port, and had consequently effected additional insurance on their consignments at very high rates. Well, after all our dangers and the buffetings the ship had received, we arrived in Albert dock in Liverpool after a passage of fifty-six days.

"Capt. Nye was so well pleased with the capabilities of Simpson, the second mate, that he complimented me for having such good judgment in selecting him, and made him a present of a patent lever English silver watch with a suitable inscription on it as a token of his regard.

"Now I'll tell you a plan that I have evolved in my mind, which, if you will agree to and accept, will be very satisfactory to me in the present, while it will be beneficial to you when we arrive in San Francisco."

"What plan is that, Captain?"

"You listen and I'll tell you. I find that several of my crew are nothing more than sloop sailors. Good enough to pull and haul about the decks but not good for anything when it comes to working aloft. When they get above the maintop it is all they can do to hold on with both hands, and therefore they are unable to do the necessary work. This, combined with the additional labor which the leaking of the ship has imposed on all hands, is becoming hard on the whole crew. In looking over the list of consignees I found your name and saw that the amount of your freight is one hundred and fifty-four dollars. That amount you will have to pay when we arrive in San Francisco before you can get the order for your goods. Now, as I have said, I find that another man to take hold and work will be a great advantage to me, and I know that you are not as contented as you would be if you had something to do. You are a sailor and I think if you will take hold and work you will be far more contented. My plan is this: as your cabin passage is paid that you continue in the cabin; that you turn to, stand watch, hand, reef and steer and help to work the ship, but do no other work, such as working on the rigging or mending sails. Your wages shall be thirty dollars per month from this time until we arrive in San Francisco. This is a good chance for you and you had better agree to it, and by this afternoon you can come into the lower cabin and give me your answer."

The captain then went aft and left me to cogitate over his proposition. I knew that he was anxious to enlist me in his service, and it was for that reason that he seemed to unbend himself in my company. I thought of the words of Shakespeare: "He bends the pregnant hinges of the knee, that thrift may follow fawning." However that may have been I felt that the offer was an advantageous one for me, and I accordingly went to the captain and told him that I was willing to go to work. "Well," said he, "I'm glad of it. You needn't sign the articles, but simply report to Mr. Bryson, in whose watch I place you."

I went into the cabin, changed my clothes, went out on deck and reported to the second mate, whose watch it was, that I was ready for duty. "Well, young fellow," said he, "the old man (the captain is always called the old man, though he be a boy) has told me that he has shipped you for the balance of the voyage, and I'm blamed glad of it, for three of the men in my watch are nothing but sloop sailors and when I send 'em aloft to do anything it seems to be all they can do is to hold on with tooth and toe-nail to keep from falling overboard. They grab the shrouds so hard that they squeeze the tar right out of 'em. They may do well enough on board of a Grand Bank fisherman, but I'm blamed if they are of much use here when they get above the bulwarks. As the old man has put you in my watch you may begin by laying aloft and loosing the fore royal." "Aye, aye, sir," I answered, and proceeded to obey the first order that I had received on board the ship "Samson."

After I had come down from aloft and the royal had been set, the second mate came to me and said, "Well, I think this is more nateral for you to do, for it is what you was brought up to, than it was for you to stand around with them Johnny Crapauds trying to learn to speak their jaw-breaking lingo. I can say I've been to sea nigh on to thirty years, man and boy, and have never been in any port where I didn't get along with plain United States English. If my language wasn't understood my money would speak for me, and I could get all the grub and all the grog that I wanted so long as I had the money to pay for it, I tell you, young feller, there's nothing that furiners understand quicker than money."

In my next watch on deck I took my first trick at the wheel, and Mr. Bryson praised me for being a good helmsman.

November first, lat. 28 17 N., long. 40 25 W. The weather was now very pleasant and we expected to soon strike the northeast trade winds. On this day we had the first view of a flying fish seen during the voyage. A flying fish is from ten to fifteen inches in length and about three inches around the thickest part of the body. It has immense dorsal fins, which it spreads when it emerges from the ocean, and sustains itself in the air for a minute or two while it skims along just above the surface of the water. When it emerges from the water it shoots out with great force at an angle of twenty-five degrees and the momentum carries it for a distance of two hundred feet or more, when it enters the water without making a ripple. The flying fish does not fly. It acquires all its propelling force in the water, and sustains itself in the air by its dorsal fins, which it outspreads but does not move them at all while out of the water. When the power acquired in the water is exhausted it has to re-enter its native element. It skims the water but does not fly.

This reminds me of the Cape Cod lad who went on a sea voyage of more than two years' duration. When he returned to his home he recounted many of his adventures to his mother: How he had been on a sea where he had seen fishes fly in the air, and on a sea that was red in color and how one very calm day they had to cast anchor to keep the ship from drifting. When the breeze sprung up they hove up the anchor and to their surprise they found a chariot wheel hanging to one of the flukes of the anchor. The good lady replied: "Zenas, my son, I believe the story about the chariot wheel hanging to one of the flukes of the anchor, because the Bible tells us how Pharaoh's hosts pursued the children of Israel with horses and chariots and were all engulfed in the Red Sea. But when you tell me that you have seen fishes flying I can't believe it."

As flying fish never bite at a baited hook we tried the

stratagem of lashing a tarpaulin about twelve feet square to the lee main shrouds, after dark, and hanging a lighted lantern on the inboard side of it. The light attracted the fish as they emerged from the water on the windward side and shot directly for the light, where they encountered the canvas and dropped down on deck, from whence they were picked up by the sailors, who got the cook to fry them the next morning, in return for which favor the sailors split stove wood for him.

November 8th. We were now well in the tropics and the northeast trades were blowing a good six-knot breeze. Lat. 23 15 N., long. 31 05 W. We were now steering southsou'west to pass Cape Saint Roque, as the captain found that the leak had somewhat increased and that he would have to put into Rio de Janeiro.

I could see that the discipline on the ship was very lax. The captain passed his time mostly in the lower cabin courting the rosy god, and for many nights at a time would not put his head above the cabin companion-way. Even during the day he would seldom pay that attention to the sailing of the ship that I had observed other captains do with whom I had sailed. It is an old saying that, "A careless captain makes careless mates."

As I have said before, Mr. Cranston, the first mate, looked more like a lawyer's clerk than he did like a seaman. When he would have the first watch on deck, which is from 8 P. M. to 12 midnight, he would pass his time chatting and giggling with the lady passengers, to the serious neglect of his duties, allowing the man at the wheel to become so careless as to keep the ship yawing about two or three points from her course, thereby losing much distance, and when the ship was close hauled the careless man at the wheel would bring her up till all the sails would be shivering and then pay her off four or five points. This makes a great difference in the sailing of a ship, and of course it prolongs the voyage. He was effeminate and simpering. He exactly filled the description given by Shakespeare as one "that capers nimbly in the lady's chamber to the lascivious pleasing of a lute." He told me that he had been educated at Wilbraham Academy, near Springfield, Mass., and it was said of him that he was a very expert navigator. A friend of his, a passenger on board, said that Cranston could navigate a ship from the Atlantic through the Gut of Canso into the Gulf of St. Lawrence without seeing the land, providing he could get an observation of sun or moon. But in seamanship he was wofully deficient and really indifferent.

On the other hand, the second mate, Mr. Bryson, was a thorough seaman, could cut a gang of standing rigging as skillfully as any master rigger that ever took a measurement, but in navigation he was a tyro. He could rig a ship and he could sail her, but in navigating her he couldn't handle the "hog yoke," as the sailors call the quadrant, with any degree of skill. He could barely work out the latitude. The mates reminded me of the nursery rhyme:

"There was Jack Sprat, who ate no fat,
 His wife, she ate no lean, sir;
 Between the two, without ado,
 They licked the platter clean, sir."

What with the splendid capacity of the first mate as a navigator and the thorough knowledge of the working of a ship by the second mate, if the captain had been less bibulous and more energetic, the ship would have been much better managed, but as things were going on board in so loose and careless manner it was evident to any observing person that we were destined to make a long, tedious voyage. I will here illustrate what a good, attentive captain can do on board of a ship under way.

The ship "Flying Cloud," built in East Boston by Donald McKay, 1851, sailed from New York in 1851, commanded by Capt. Cressy. She made the passage to San Francisco in eighty-nine days and twenty hours, a distance of eighteen thousand miles, around Cape Horn, besides the devious distance sailed when the wind was adverse; and during all this voyage it was said that she never parted a ropeyarn. When she arrived in San Francisco the mercantile community was astonished, as nothing in the sailing line had ever before approached such a feat. It was told by members of the ship's crew that from the day that the ship sailed from New York until she was anchored in San Francisco, that Capt. Cressy had not allowed a single watch of four hours to pass without coming on deck at least once during the watch. The mate in charge of the watch was especially directed to con the helm, to study every variation of the wind and to trim the sails accordingly, and from such close application came such very brilliant results.

In this port Capt. Cressy and his ship became the cynosure of all eyes. A big restaurant which was about to be opened was named the "Flying Cloud." A clothing store just opened, was called the "Flying Cloud" clothing store; and to cap the climax an enthusiastic old sailor, who stood on the corner of Sansome and Halleck streets, waiting for odd jobs of hauling, caused his hand-cart to be painted a bright green, and a legend painted on the tailboard bearing these words: "Flying Cloud looking for a job."

On the second voyage of the "Flying Cloud" she beat her record by one hour, making the voyage in eighty-nine days and nineteen hours. To Capt. Cressy and his ship belongs the honor of the greatest performance in sailing that is known in the maritime world. When I contrast the achievement of this ship with the lax and slovenly management of the "Samson," which vessel took seventy-five days to reach Rio de Janeiro, under very favorable conditions, I feel convinced that to make a quick passage, very much depends upon the close application of the captain to the proper sailing of his ship.

November 15th. We are now having light winds, lat. 18 12 N., long. 30 22 W., weather warm. We were daily approached by schools of porpoises, and they would often sport around the ship and come right under her bows. We had a sailor that had once been on a whaling voyage in a schooner from Provincetown, Cape Cod, and he claimed to be a good harpooner. The chief mate caused a harpoon to be rigged, and used a coil of rattling stuff for a line; it was placed in the waist, on the lee side, and the end passed outside the forerigging to the bow, and lashed to the harpoon. When everything was ready the whaleman, whose name was Amaziah Nickerson, took the harpoon, went out to the martingale and lashed himself to it, so as to have the free use of his hands, and stand ready for a chance to strike a porpoise. The chance soon occurred, for a porpoise came within range and Amaziah threw the harpoon with such force and precision that it passed clear through the body of the monster. As soon as the porpoise was struck the mate ordered the helm to be put hard down and eased up the head sheets and the ship came up into the wind, which stopped her headway. In the meantime the porpoise was struggling fiercely, but without avail. The struggle soon ceased, and the porpoise was hauled alongside. Amaziah was placed in the bight of a rope and lowered over the side; he then placed a running bowline over the flukes of the monster and it was hoisted on board with a watch tackle. When it was stretched on deck all the passengers gathered around, and all of them expressed unbounded wonder at the sight of the denizen of the mighty deep. Its weight was reckoned to be about three hundred and fifty pounds. Sailors often call them sea hogs. The monster was immediately opened and its liver taken out. It was then 9:30 A. M. The captain ordered the cook to prepare the liver for a special luncheon for the ladies and have it ready by eleven o'clock. The cook cut the liver into slices and washed it in salt and water, after which he wiped it dry, dredged it with dry flour and fried it with slices of bacon. The odor of the frying liver and bacon that issued from the galley carried the memory of the young passengers from the interior of Pennsylvania back to their father's farm in hog killing time, and excited their gustatory organs to such a degree that it caused the saliva to exude from their mouths and trickle down their chins in tiny rivulets. The eight ladies on board enjoyed the novel dish of fried porpoise liver and bacon, and declared that it was the most delicious morsel that they had eaten in many a day. Then the body of the porpoise was stripped of the blubber, which was tried out for oil for the forecastle lamps, and the meat was cut into strips, parboiled in salt and water and wiped dry. After this it was mixed with a small proportion of salt pork and chopped fine. It was then seasoned with dried sage and summer savory, pepper and salt, and rolled into small balls, covered with dry flour, and then fried in a pan of hot fat, and served piping hot. It must be said that to us it tasted as palatable as a dish of Fulton market sausage meat ever tasted to us when in New York. We all liked it so well that when the supply—which lasted two days—was exhausted we, like Oliver Twist, asked for more of the same kind. The French passengers were so well pleased that one of them sent a bottle of brandy, by the cabin boy, to Amaziah as a reward for his prowess. After this feast everything moved along in the old groove.

November 19th, lat. 14 24 N., long. 31 16 W. We expected to reach the equator in a few days and the sailors began to talk about having a visit from Neptune. After discussing the subject they resolved to ask permission from the captain to enact the part, and solicited Mr. Bryson, the second mate, to act as their advocate. Mr. Bryson accordingly approached the captain upon the subject, and strengthened his argument by saying that in nearly all the ships in which he had crossed the line the Neptune drama was allowed to be enacted, and never had resulted in anything unpleasant. The captain said he was willing if the weather should permit, but there should be no tar used in the lather, nor should he allow a rusty iron hoop for a razor—but a wooden razor instead. All these preliminaries being arranged, the sailors commenced at once to prepare for the grand occasion. Mr. Bryson furnished an old topgallant studdingsail from which they made three cloaks and trimmed them with strands of Manila ropeyarns, and painted them green, to resemble sea weed. They also made three pairs of canvas sandals and painted them green also. They made three pairs of leggings of red flannel, which were to be tied around their ankles. A Russian fur cap was fitted with a band of sheet brass, and two bands, crossing each other, over the top of the cap, altogether resembling a coronet, which was to be worn by

Neptune. A sailor named Stanwood, possessing a basso profundo voice, was to enact the part of the sea king. His two satellites were to have wigs made of Manila strands. Their faces were to be daubed with yellow ochre.

November the twenty-first proved a propitious day for the enactment of the great drama, it being bright and pleasant, with a three-knot breeze. The word was passed around the ship during the forenoon that Neptune might board the ship during the day. One o'clock was the time at which the passengers would be in the cabin taking their dinner. Mr. Bryson had kindly consented to act as master of ceremonies. By observation at 12 meridian we were in lat. 8 23 N., long. 31 05 W. The wind was abaft the beam; the ship was sliding along about four knots; the second mate was in charge of the deck, as the chief mate was in the cabin taking his dinner.

At 1:15 P. M. a stentorian voice called out, "Ship ahoy!" "Hello!" answered the second mate through the speaking trumpet, which had been purposely placed at hand. "What ship is that?" "The 'Samson,' from Philadelphia." "Heave back your maintopsail, as Neptune is coming aboard." "Aye, aye, sir." Then the chief mate, who had come on deck, ordered the helm to be put hard down, the mainsail to be hauled up, and the maintopsail to be hove aback.

The passengers, who had heard the ship hailed, apparently from a distance, hurried out of the cabin and saw a sight that astonished them and caused some of them to blanch with fright. There they saw before them Neptune, dressed in his royal robes of green cloak and red breeches, with crown on his head and scepter or trident in his hand, attended by his two satellites, one on each side; while one carried an immense steel-colored (made of wood) razor, the other one carried a bucket and a huge brush made of oakum lashed to a stick for a handle. The attendants had green cloaks like their master and a head covering of what appeared to be seaweed. They marched with measured step as far aft as the mainmast, where they were met by the chief

NEPTUNE BOARDING THE SHIP.

mate, who raised his cap to Neptune, the monarch of the ocean. Then spoke Neptune, "I know that you have a number of novices on board, who must be inducted into the mysteries of my dominion. Bring a list of their names, and state the occupation of each." "Aye, aye, sir," answered the mate.

The list had, of course, been previously prepared, and it was handed to Mr. Bryson, master of ceremonies. Neptune ordered him to read the list and call out the names, which he did in the following order:

Deidrich Cluffwater, farmer;
Hans Van Bokkelin, farmer;
Dick Grimes, cabin boy;
Benj. F. Jackson, compositor;
Edward Brainard, student;
John Edgar, pressman;
Mons. Dubardie, embassador;
Mons. Bayard, soldier;
Mons. Bushey, Perruquier to his majesty Louis Phillip;
Mons. Guizot, gentleman.

The above embraced the list of those persons that were to be inducted into the family of Neptune, and to be known thereafter as the "Sons of Neptune."

Preparations were now made for the shaving of the novices. The half of a large water cask was placed near the mainmast and was filled with salt water. Across the cask was placed a capstan-bar to serve as a seat for the candidate. A bucket was used in which the lather of soap and grease had been already prepared. One of the attendants used the mop, while the other one wielded the wooden razor, which was painted steel color. Neptune stood majestically with cloak and crown, holding his trident in his right hand. The master of ceremonies led forward the person whose name was first on the list, Deidrich Cluffwater. A more disconsolate looking young fellow I never looked upon before. They seated him on the edge of the big half cask, with a capstan-bar for a seat. One of Neptune's attendants held him to the seat while the other one plied the brush or mop with no gentle hand. Whenever the victim opened his mouth to breathe the mop was thrust into it, which caused him to splutter and spit. When the lather had been applied, the attendant laid the mop down and held the victim while the barber wielded the razor with a great deal of vigor and some roughness. After the shaving was completed the two operators held the victim by the shoulders and soused him backwards into the cask of water, and then raised him up half smothered. Then they wiped him off with a canvas towel, which was as painful as the shave.

Now came the time for Neptune to speak. He told the novice to stand up, which he had to do as the two satellites were holding him. His majesty propounded the following questions:

Ques. Do you solemnly swear that you will never eat brown bread when you can get white? Ans. I swear.

Ques. Do you solemnly swear that you will never kiss the maid when you can kiss the mistress? Ans. I swear.

Ques. Do you solemnly swear that you will not drink water when you can get wine? Ans. I swear.

"Very well," said his Majesty, at the same time laying his scepter gently across the shoulders of the candidate; "I pronounce you a true Son of Neptune by adoption, and hereby invest you with all the privileges appertaining to the sons of the King of the Sea."

Then the master of ceremonies escorted him aft, saying at the same time, " Old Neptune has let you into his family easier than he did me. When I first crossed the line, years ago, he came on board our ship, and put me and three other young fellers through the exercises, and done it without gloves; you bet he did. He had his barbers to make a lather of soap, slush out of the galley coppers, and tar, which was rubbed all over my face; then they scraped me with a razor made of hoop iron. After they got through with me, my face was as raw as a piece of beef."

Cluffwater was glad to be liberated, and soon appeared on deck in clean clothes, to see his friend Van Bokkelin put through the same process.

The ladies being aware that the motto on the escutcheon of Neptune was: "Ladies admitted free," and feeling the security of immunity, enjoyed the novel performance, and laughed until the tears coursed down their cheeks.

The next to be operated upon was Van Bokkelin. He was escorted by the master of ceremonies and was subjected to the same process as Cluffwater had been. After this came Dick Grimes, for whom I felt a sort of pity, because sailors charge cabin boys with being tale bearers, carrying tales from the forecastle to the captain in the cabin. The master of ceremonies told him to come with him, but Dick, instead, began to run towards the cabin; then Mr. Bryson called two of the sailors aft and ordered them to take the boy by the nape of the neck and the slack of his breeches and convey him before Neptune, which the sailors at once proceeded to do, con amore, while Dick howled and kicked vigorously, but without avail, as he was placed on the shaving stool and taken charge of by the two satellites. Just then, from an unexpected quarter, arose a friend and advocate for Dick. This was sweet little Blanche, the four-year old daughter of the captain. She stood on the roof of the cabin, and with flashing eyes called out: "Go away! you bad mans, let poor Dick alone! I'll tell my papa on you, and he'll give you a hard whipping." But Neptune's attendants were obdurate, and proceeded to lather and shave Dick in a manner that proved that they meant to make the most of their opportunity. "Dick, don't cry," said Blanche; "stop! you bad mans." After the barbers had concluded their labors they placed the boy before Neptune, who made him take the usual oath with the following addenda: "Do you solemnly swear that you'll never more carry tales from the forecastle to the cabin?" "I swear." "Go, now, you imp of mischief."

After the three first had been duly shaved, the chief mate came to Mr. Bryson and held a short conference, the result of which was that Mr. Bryson informed Neptune that the balance of the novices desired to obtain exemption from the ordeal undergone by the others, by laying gifts at his feet. His Majesty acquiesced in the plan, thereby showing that royalty is never known to refuse a good thing when it is offered in a proper spirit. The first one to come forward with his offering was Benj. F. Jackson, who brought a bound volume of the "Philadelphia Ledger," that had been presented to him in that office when he withdrew to go to California. The next was John Edgar, the pressman, who presented a fine copy of Burns' Poems, presented to him in the printing house where he had served his apprenticeship. The four Frenchmen brought each a bottle of old cognac brandy and placed them at the feet of his Majesty. Edward Brainard, student, was exempted by reason of his misfortunes. After this was completed, which took about one hour, Mr. Bryson requested all the passengers to withdraw into the cabin. After the deck was cleared, Neptune and his attendants at once dove down into the forecastle; the ship was filled away on her course and everything looked as natural as before Neptune had appeared. I must say that Capt. Blanchard had behaved handsomely, for during the whole ceremony he never appeared on deck once, thereby giving Neptune and his attendants a chance to have full play. An hour after this, Stanwood and his two aids, having divested themselves of their fantastic rig, came on deck to resume their duties, and really, any one that didn't know about it would never suspect that Neptune and Stanwood were one and the same person.

During the afternoon I noticed that the two cooks appeared to be extra busy. The steward told me that Stanwood had given him one of the four bottles of cognac, therefore he was going to reciprocate by giving the sailors a treat of mince turnovers for their supper. Mince turnovers, on board of a ship, are made of salt beef, chopped fine and mixed with three times the quantity of boiled dried apples, a little dried orange peel, allspice, and molasses to taste, and a taste of vinegar. Dough cut into small sections after it is rolled thin. Put one spoonful of the mince in each section, bring the edges together, put each one in a frying pan, filled with hot fat, and fry them brown. When one side is fried turn the pie over—hence the name, "fried turnovers." In the absence of luxuries on board of a ship such simple dishes are a great boon to the sailor. I saw one of the sailors receive from the cook a big panful of turnovers, which he carried forward for their supper. It was our first watch on deck that night and I saw the steward and the two cooks hob-nobbing together and discussing the episode of Neptune's visit. The head cook, who was an American-African, said that the affair of that day was one of the pleasantest and beautifulest that he ever seed. The steward, who was an Englishman, said that it was too tame and insipid altogether. Said he: "It takes an English crew on an English ship to give force and character to Neptune's visit, where real tar is used, and real hoop iron is used for a razor. You may brag all you like about your Brother Jonathan but it takes John Bull to do things in ship-shape and Bristol fashion, in everything that he undertakes." The steward was a true type of the all sufficient supercilious British sailor.

We were now in the torrid zone with wind light and very hot weather. At noon time the heat was so intense that the pitch oozed out of the deck seams.

On November twenty-second the steward informed the mate that the fresh water was reduced down to six casks out of fifty which we had on deck when we left Philadelphia. The fact was that the passengers had used the fresh water in a most prodigal manner as if there was a never-failing spring to drawn from. The sailors seeing how freely the passengers were helping themselves—and washing their clothes—were not slow in following their example; the consequence being that we found ourselves in the tropics, with the air as hot as an oven when the wind was moderate, and we had only six full casks of water on deck. It is true, there were two iron tanks between decks containing five hundred gallons each, but this was a reserve supply in case the deck should be swept by a sea. The captain was informed of the condition of affairs, which caused him to storm and roar at the mates because of their neglect, and scolded the steward for his extravagance. He ordered the second mate to take charge of the water and have each day pumped out of the cask sufficient to supply each man with two quarts of water per day—one quart to drink, one quart for coffee and tea. This severe measure need not have been adopted if the captain had exercised that supervision and discipline that causes everything to go on smoothly on board of a ship.

With cabin passengers the mate cannot or does not assert that superiority that is essential in the maintenance of discipline. From the day on which we passed Cape Henlopen, Mr. Cranston, the first mate, seemed oblivious to everything but standing his watch, and navigating the ship, and paying devout attention to the lady passengers, while Mr. Bryson, the second mate, would take a sailor to task sooner about the waste of a fathom of spunyarn than he would if he saw him take a bucket of fresh water wherewith to wash his clothes. "But," you ask, "where was the captain all this time?" He was in the cabin worshiping at the shrine of the rosy god Bacchus. This was a plain illustration of the old adage, which says: "When the cat is away the mice will play."

The captain now determined to put into Rio de Janeiro, as the ship leaked copiously and we were short of fresh water, and therefore not in a condition to venture around Cape Horn! It was now November 26th. Our position at 12 meridian was lat. 1 15 south, long. 29 30 west; wind E. N. E. The ship was brought a point to the southward in order that we might weather Cape Saint Roque, in lat. 5 28 S., long. 35 17 W. Every one on board the ship now began to discuss the captain's change of plan of the voyage. Some of them deplored the necessity of putting into Rio, fearing that the gold in California would be all dug up before we would arrive there. Others of the passengers were delighted with the prospect of seeing a new country and once more placing their feet on dry land. The wind was now freshening and the ship moved through the water at a race-horse speed.

November 27th at 2 P. M. we sighted Cape Saint Roque, bearing south-southwest, distant about twenty miles. The sight of land produced a very animating effect upon all the passengers. The ladies ranged themselves on the quarter-deck and each one in turn took a view of the distant land through the spy-glass, while the young men laughed and skipped about the deck as if they had become boys again. The Frenchmen opened a few extra bottles of claret for themselves and became quite loquacious. The interdiction on the free use of fresh water for drinking purposes was removed, and an air of cheerfulness pervaded the whole company on the ship.

Thanksgiving Day was now near, a day hallowed by the Pilgrims who landed on Plymouth Rock in 1620, when—

The breaking waves dashed high
On a stern and rock-bound coast,
And the woods against the stormy sky
Their giant branches tossed.

The heavy night hung dark
The hills and water o'er,
When a band of pilgrims moored their bark
On the wild New England shore.

Thanksgiving Day has ever been a day of special devotion and of feasting in all New England since that day in November when Providence had blessed them with an abundant harvest, after having suffered drought and hunger for two years after their first landing. The fore part of the day is devoted to divine worship, after which is inaugurated the grand feast of the year. From this beginning has Thanksgiving Day been perpetuated, and is held precious by every son of New England, wherever his lot may be cast. The family on that day, though widely separated, gather under the parental roof and pass the day in family communion. Nor is the stranger neglected on that day, but is supplied with ample quantity of food, not omitting a generous piece of New England mince pie.

An opulent merchant named Jonathan Bourne, of New Bedford, Mass., some years ago sent a liberal sum of money to the Selectmen of Sandwich, Mass., with a request that they buy an ample supply of turkey and also a sufficient quantity of cider to supply one bottle each to every inmate of the town farm on Thanksgiving Day. In concluding his letter he said: "It is my desire that the poor and wretched of my native town shall forget their misery on Thanksgiving Day." This noble act of Mr. Bourne will be remembered when his wealth and his business enterprise will have been forgotten.

Capt. Blanchard was from Maine and Mr. Cranston was from Massachusetts, yet neither one of them mentioned a word about the approaching Thanksgiving Day. The steward was an Englishman, and the two darkey cooks were from Maryland, therefore they wouldn't know Thanksgiving Day even if they saw it standing before them. One of the sailors named Miles Standish Bradstreet, who hailed from Gardiner, Maine, said that he had sailed for many years in lumber drogers between Portland and the West Indies, and never in all that time had Thanksgiving Day been allowed to pass without proper recognition, neither at sea nor in port—always being observed with extra fare fore and aft.

The last Thursday in November arrived, which is usually the day appointed by the Governor of each State as a holiday; but on board of our ship there was no sign to denote the event. Neither in the galley nor pantry was there any signs of unusual activity. At 12 meridian, the mate, who had been observing the sun with his sextant, sung out, "Twelve o'clock!" The captain, who for a wonder was on the quarter-deck, said to the man at the wheel, "Make it so." "Aye, aye, sir," and he struck eight bells. The man on the lookout forward responded by striking eight bells on the ship's bell and ran to the forecastle gangway and called out, "Starboard watch ahoy! eight bells." The starboard watch came on deck. Two of the sailors went to the galley to receive the dinner for all hands forward. The cook gave them one kit of beef, one kit of pork, one bake-pan full of dandyfunk. Potatoes were long since exhausted.

Dandyfunk is a dish composed of navy biscuit soaked in water, mashed with a pestle, mixed with fat taken from the coppers in which the meat is boiled, sweetened with molasses and flavored with allspice, then put into a pan and baked in the oven. It isn't a very high-toned dish, but in the absence of something better it is very palatable to a sailor.

The crew sat down on the deck, as it was usual for them to do in pleasant weather, and ate their dinner. While the dinner was being eaten Miles Standish Bradstreet, who claimed to be a lineal descendant of Capt. Miles Standish, the Pilgrim warrior, arose from the deck, holding a big beef bone in one hand, and holding it up high he delivered the following elegy on the ox:

> From Saccarap to Portland pier
> I've dragged lumber for many a year;
> After a long and sore abuse,
> They packed me down for sailors' use;
> They cook me up and pick my bones,
> And throw the rest to Davy Jones.

And suiting the action to the words, he threw the bone over the weather side of the ship. The French passengers were curiously watching the performance, and when Doctor Doriot explained it all to them they laughed heartily, and one of them sent a bottle of cognac brandy to the sailors while another passenger filled a bread tray heaping full of sweet biscuits from his private stores and sent it forward. Thus, after all, the sailors had a jolly Thanksgiving dinner.

At 1 o'clock the passengers sat down to their dinner of salt beef, salt pork, boiled hominy, pickles, rice pudding and cheese. Although it was Thanksgiving Day there was nothing said in commemoration of the Pilgrim holiday, as most of the passengers were from Pennsylvania or else from the South, where Thanksgiving Day was unknown. It remained for Abraham Lincoln, the Christian President, to proclaim Thanksgiving Day a national holiday throughout the length and breadth of this glorious land, that acknowledges a divine supervision over all nations.

Having weathered Cape Saint Roque, our course was changed to more westerly, and as the wind was about E. S. E., we were going free with topmast-studdingsails set. On this day a number of dolphins were seen swimming near our quarter. Capt. Blanchard told Mr. Bryson to bring the grains, also a sea-leadline for a lanyard. Mr. Bryson fitted the grains to the staff, lashed the lanyard to it, and then took it aft to the captain. The captain grasped the grains and stood near the taffrail watching for a chance. The fish would approach until they were almost under the ship's counter, and then suddenly dart off to a distance. After a time the captain saw his opportunity; he threw the grains and lo, it struck a dolphin. There was great excitement on the quarter-deck among the passengers. The fish darted in every direction and turned up its sides, showing the most beautiful colors imaginable. After its struggles had somewhat subsided it was hauled on deck by the willing aid of the passengers. It measured all of five feet in length. The ladies congratulated the captain for the accuracy of his throw and he seemed as proud as a peacock because of his achievement. The dolphin laid on deck twisting and turning, while his skin showed every color of the rainbow.

The captain ordered the cook to clean it and fry it. He handed him a silver half-dollar piece and told him to let it remain in the frying-pan while the fish was cooking, and when the fish was cooked to fetch the half dollar to him so that he might note its color. After the fish was fried the cook returned the half dollar to the captain, and it had become as black as a piece of coal. The captain became convinced that the fish was poisonous, and ordered it to be thrown overboard at once. Thus the ladies lost their anticipated feast of fried dolphin.

The reason of the fish being in a poisonous condition was because the bottom of the ocean over which we were then sailing was heavily impregnated with copper ore, and the ocean weeds on which the fishes feed contained the verdigris that exudes from the copper ore, hence whoever eats such fish becomes poisoned.

The weather now showed signs of an approaching change. Scuds were flying to the eastward and at the setting of the sun it was partially obscured by heavy clouds that appeared to be charged with rain. The wind was still from E. S. E., while our course was S. W. by S. Toward midnight the wind died away and the ship lay moving with the gentle undulations of the ocean, while her sails flapped helplessly against the masts. At 6 A. M. it began to rain in gentle drops while the sky was invisible on account of the heavy clouds. We took the two lower studdingsails and spread one over the upper cabin deck and the other over the longboat on top of the forward house, in order that we might catch all the fresh water possible wherewith to wash our persons and also our clothes. The rain now came down in torrents and the wind began to increase, but as it was still comparatively moderate we did not shorten sail. We filled two water casks with rain water and were still busy when the alarm was given with startling emphasis: "A waterspout! A water-spout!" We stopped dipping the fresh water at once and looked in the direction indicated by the alarmist, and to our consternation we saw an enormous water-spout off our starboard quarter, about six hundred feet off, and moving with a rotary motion towards the ship.

The captain, who stood on the quarter-deck, ordered the mate to fetch up the swivel cannon from its locker in the lower cabin. The mate called two men and they went down below and quickly returned with the cannon, which was always kept loaded for emergencies. It was taken forward and shipped into the socket on the top of the samson post. The touch-hole was protected by a heavy apron of painted canvas. The mate went to the cabin and soon ran out with a lighted fuse, which he shielded under his oilcloth coat. He stood ready for the word of command. The water-spout was moving with the wind towards the ship with a threatening swirl. It was now within two hundred feet of the ship, and it looked awe inspiring. It looked like an immense balloon when it is inflated and about to be loosened from its moorings. Every man on board the ship was on deck, re-

"Deep calleth unto deep at the voice of thy water-spouts."—Psalms 42, 7th verse.

gardless of the pouring rain, and each seemed to be holding his breath with fright. This brought to my mind the words of holy writ: "Deep calleth unto deep at the voice of thy water-spouts."—Psalms, 42, 7th verse. The suspense was horrible. All at once the captain thundered out: "Fire!" Whiz, bang, went the charge and sent the one pound iron ball into the water-spout, which collapsed into a seething, swirling, foaming mass of lumpy ocean. It appeared to have contained a sufficient quantity of water to have submerged the ship twenty feet deep. We were saved. I felt at that moment that I could forgive Capt. Blanchard for all his previous shortcomings, for had the water-spout struck the ship in its entirety it would have sunk her there and then.

After the collapse of the water-spout a discussion arose between Doctor Doriot, who was educated in Girard College, and Mr. Shorb, the Virginia lawyer, who had been educated at Yale, where most of the young Southerners were graduated at that time. Doctor Doriot remarked that the aim of Mr. Cranston had been very accurate, for the ball had penetrated the water-spout, and thereby destroyed the suction, and hence the collapse. Mr. Shorb said that such was not the case. He said that the explosion of the powder had caused a concussion in the air and consequently had destroyed the entity of the water-spout and caused its total collapse. The two collegians continued their wrangling in the cabin to the annoyance of the other passengers, who were satisfied with the result without caring about hairsplitting theories.

Towards noon the weather began to clear up and the wind changed to the northwest, giving us a fair wind. By the noon observation our latitude was 9 85 south, longitude 37 40 west, making the distance from Rio de Janeiro 950 miles; course, S. S. W.

It was now the fourth day of December and we began to look forward with pleasure to an early arrival in Rio de Janeiro. We sighted a vessel occasionally, steering south like ourselves, which made it seem very companionable from the fact that when at sea there is nothing in sight but sky and water and the only living thing to be seen is the poor little "mother Carey's chickens," which little creatures become endeared to the sailor by their constant companionship on the wide, lonely ocean. Mother Carey's chickens are little ocean birds that very much resemble the little swallows that are so common around the barn on shore. They follow a ship constantly, in sunshine and in storm, and dart around her like little guardian angels to look out for the welfare of poor Jack. The mate now ordered the masts to be scraped, the rigging tarred down, the bulwarks to be painted, and everything on board to be made sightly and presentable. Mr. Bryson was now as busy as a hen with twenty chickens. He kept the men hard at it from 8 o'clock in the morning until noon, and from 1 P. M. until 5 P. M. As to me, they never called upon me to do more than what I agreed to do. That was to "work ship," take my regular trick at the wheel and my turn at the lookout.

Capt. Blanchard again sent for young Brainard, who, in obedience to the summons, went into the lower cabin, where the captain detained him for nearly an hour. When he returned on deck I saw that he looked flushed and troubled. The first opportunity he had he told me that the captain had demanded of him that he turn over to him his father's papers, including the bills of lading, as he, being but a boy, was not a fit custodian for them. He declined to yield to the captain's demand; he then told him that he was but an interloper on board of his ship, and for that reason he would put him ashore the very moment that the anchor was dropped in Rio de Janeiro. This threat produced a very depressing effect on the poor youth and caused the tears to run down his cheeks. I pitied the poor fellow and tried to console him with cheering words. I then thought of the poetic couplet:

"Man's inhumanity to man,
Makes countless thousands mourn."

The weather was now very warm, and the wind a whole sail breeze from east to east nor'east, and our course was south southwest. December tenth, by observation at noon, was lat. 11 17 S., long. 41 03 W. All hands and the passengers availed themselves of the chance to use the rain water, which we had saved during the rainstorm, and the decks presented the appearance of a floating laundry. We washed our sea-going clothes and scrubbed our persons to get off a coating of salt about a quarter of an inch thick, as we had been deprived of our fresh water privileges for a long time. The passengers now began to practice the tonsorial art upon one another—cutting the hair, trimming the whiskers of more than sixty days' growth, shaving and shampooing. Our fare at the table began to improve, as the steward and the cooks knew that they would have a respite from their labors for a time after we arrived in Rio. We had for dinner, daily, besides beef and pork, baked beans, boiled hominy, tapioca pudding enriched with eggs, and cornstarch pudding with cheese. For supper, dried beef sliced, hot biscuits, dried apple sauce, and fine doughnuts.

December eighteenth the cry of "land ho!" from a man aloft. "Where away?" sung out the mate. "Three points on the lee-bow, sir!" "Very well," said the mate. The captain was called, who at once came on deck. He and the mate held a conference, and they decided that the land in sight was Cape Frio, lat. 23 01 S., long. 41 59 W. The captain ordered the man at the wheel to keep her off two points. "Aye, aye, sir!" responded the man, at the same time swaying the helm to port. The weather braces were ordered to be checked in and the ship felt the impulse of the favoring breeze and accelerated her speed considerably. After dark we sighted Cape Frio light. The captain ordered the mates to place two men on the look-out, as we were in the track of vessels that were bound into Rio. The passengers stood around on deck until eight bells, discussing the probable length of our detention in Rio. One gentleman from Pennsylvania who was on board with his wife, declared that if he ever got a chance to put his feet on dry land once more that he would not go to sea again with such a captain, even if he and his wife had to work their passage back to their home.

But the gentleman had no occasion to do so for the reason that he had ample means, and afterwards he left the ship in Rio and took passage for himself and wife in the ship "Ducalion," that touched at Rio on her way to San Francisco.

On the nineteenth we had a spanking breeze and old "Samson" was putting in her best licks. The captain had now laid aside all foolishness and staid on deck all day, watched the weather, conned the helm, and observed all that was going on. I then thought that if he had acted thus from the time that we took our departure from Cape Henlopen we would now have been well on towards Cape Horn by this time. We were overtaken by a number of vessels that were steering the same course. We were spoken by one vessel showing the Danish flag—red ground and white cross—but as there was no Dane on board our ship we couldn't understand them.

On the twentieth of December we entered the harbor of Rio de Janeiro. We went in by the Sugar Loaf—a conical rock that rises sharply out of the water and reaches up many hundred feet, and, as its name designates, in shape of a sugar loaf. Next we passed the fortresses Santa Cruz and San Juan, and sailed up towards the anchorage, and the chains having been shackled to the anchors and the lashings cast off, the order was given to take in sail. Down came the royals; down came the topgallantsails; up went the courses, down came the jib; down came the three topsails; down came the foretopmast staysail. The spanker brought the ship up to the wind and she lost her headway. "Stand by your larboard anchor!" "Aye, aye, sir!" answered the mate. As the ship reached up to the wind and began to gather sternway, the order was given: "Let go your anchor!" "Let go it is!" and way went the anchor, and whirr went the chain until the anchor struck bottom. Then the ship trended to the wind; then we were safe in Rio de Janeiro, after a tedious voyage of seventy-six days.

As I looked around the harbor with its numerous shipping, and cast my eyes towards the beautiful city before us, and as I looked around upon our leaky ship, short of provisions, short of water, an indifferent, bibulous captain, and then I felt a longing and desire to reach California by some other vessel, the beautiful verse of a hymn arose to my mind:

> " Thus far the Lord hath led me on,
> Thus far he hath prolonged my days,
> And every evening doth make known,
> Some fresh memorial of His grace."

Here we were anchored in Rio de Janeiro, lat. 23 37 23 S., long. 43 08 34 W., after a passage of seventy-six days from Philadelphia. The captain ordered his gig, which had been turned over on the upper cabin deck, and protected by a painted canvas jacket, to be put in the water alongside. This job was quickly done. The boat leaked a little, but the captain took along two men to row him ashore, and the boy Dick to bail out the water. As the captain was going over the side he ordered the mate to get the longboat off the forward house and get her into the water. It was then five o'clock. We furled the sails, and then rigged the tackles to hoist the longboat, as she was large and heavy. When everything was ready, the mate sang out, "Hoist away!" As the tackles were drawn taut, the men called to Stanwood: "Give a shanter, old boy!" And he sang the following hoisting song, which was chorused by the men:

> " The ladies like Madeira wine,
> The gents they like their brandy oh!
> So early in the morning—
> The sailor likes his bottle oh!
> His bottle oh! his bottle oh!
> The sailor likes his bottle oh!
>
> CHORUS.
> So early in the morning—
> The sailor likes his bottle oh!"

The longboat was lowered into the water, and, with a double painter, was secured astern of the ship. The captain returned on board at eight o'clock and brought off a quantity of fresh beef and sweet potatoes. The captain, immediately after he came on board, descended to the lower cabin, and was not seen again that night. Dick, the boy, said that the captain went to a big hotel and engaged accommodations for himself and family for the time that he would remain in port. We all retired early, and it was pleasant to turn into the berth and repose freed from the constant unceasing motion of the ship and the creaking of her timbers. The next morning everyone was up early. The second mate and the sailors had already commenced to wash down the decks and pumping out the ship, that leaked as much while lying at anchor as she had done when she was at sea. After the decks were washed, Mr. Bryson took his station on the topgallant forecastle and scanned the yards while they were squared by the lifts and braces. As to myself I was now relieved from any further duty. As soon as the anchor had struck bottom and the sails had been furled I became my own master again.

At eight o'clock we had breakfast of fried beef, boiled sweet potatoes, and hot biscuits. The mate told us that such of the passengers as wanted to go ashore should be ready by nine o'clock, at which time he would have one of the quarter boats ready to take us there. After breakfast I went to my chest and took out my warm weather go-ashore suit, which I had bought in Havana, Cuba, two years before. It consisted of white linen jacket, vest and trowsers, a pair of morocco shoes, and a Panama straw hat. White shirts I had a good supply of. I had in my mind the injunction of Polonius to his son Laertes, when he was about to go abroad among strangers:

> "Costly thy habit as thy purse can buy,
> But not expressed in fancy;
> Rich, not gaudy;
> For the apparel oft proclaims the man."

After I had donned my go-ashore toggery I went out on deck and there I found Mr. Bryson, good natured as usual, and smoking his after-breakfast cigar. When he saw me, he exclaimed: "Why, I declare, you look like a supercargo that is just going ashore to sell the ship's cargo to the merchants of the port. Well, young feller, 'go it while you're young, for when you're old you can't.'" The quarter boat had been lowered and as many of us as could find room got into her and were rowed ashore by two of the sailors. We arrived at a small stone jetty where the small boats landed their passengers. The lower harbor is spacious, being about ten miles from shore to shore, and its length is sixteen miles from the entrance to the head of the harbor, making it one of the safest land-locked havens in the world. When a ship calls in Rio for orders or for obtaining fresh provisions she anchors in the lower harbor, as in cove of Cork, Ireland, but when she is to load or unload then she is taken to the upper harbor, about a mile above, where it is more land-locked and where all the wharves are built. When we jumped on shore, my companions instinctively grasped one another by the hand, and offered congratulations for our safe delivery from the dangers of the mighty deep, and thanks to an overruling Providence for permitting us to again place our feet on "terra firma."

As we stepped ashore we were surrounded by a horde of swarthy Portuguese and coal-black negroes, speaking a jargon of unintelligible conglomeration of half a dozen languages. This mixture of tongues was easily accounted for when I saw the flags of most every maritime nation floating from the different ships in the harbor, who, like ourselves, had touched there either for provisions or from stress of weather, to repair damages. After we had passed through the crowd that had intercepted us at the beach, we saw a large building of two high stories, with a wide balcony surrounding the second-story, which was shaded by an awning of striped canvas, which made it look very gay and attractive. Surmounting the parapet was an immense sign bearing the legend "Hotel do Pharoux," in letters large enough to be seen from a mile distant in the harbor. As we approached the place we saw a great number of persons going in and coming out of the spacious barroom. As we approached we were accosted by a great number of California bound gold seekers, who asked what ship we had come on and how long we had been on the way. We found that we had been longer on our passage than any other vessel then in the harbor.

Our company now paired off. Mr. Cluffwater and myself went together. We found Rio to be a city that was built mostly on a level plain, which comprised the business portion. On the right from where we landed was a rise of gently ascending hills on which are built many monasteries and convents, in which the city abounds, as well as quiet residences; but the business was done in the level part of the city. After we passed the hotel we arrived in front of a building of two high stories and of very great length, with a courtyard in front in which was a large marble fountain that was throwing a jet of water that sparkled in the sun like a shower of diamonds.

This, we learned, was the palace of the Emperor. It was built of stone, like all the other buildings that we saw. It was very comfortable in outward appearance, but there was no architectural display. It might be called neat but not gaudy. At the archway of the entrance I saw a solitary sentinel pacing back and forth. No other display of military pomp did I see at that time. Adjoining the palace was the Emperor's chapel, which, although called a chapel, was in reality a large church. It had no exterior elegance, but when I visited it some days afterwards I found that the interior, architecturally and ornamentally, was very grand and magnificent. It has a vaulted roof, with a succession of arches resting on pillars fluted and gilded, giving the interior an appearance of unparalleled grandeur. The main altar was indescribably rich with images and carvings. Between the pillars were side altars dedicated to saints; portieres of gold cloth leading into the sacristy. The organ loft was immediately over the entrance. Outside the railing of the sanctuary, extending a few feet, were two elevated grand chairs for the Emperor and the Empress, with a few less conspicuous seats for his suite. The floor of the church was devoid of pews, and the grand ladies, when they attended mass, were attended by female slaves with tiny mats for their mistresses to kneel upon. All the women, when attending mass, wore a head covering called a mantilla, for Saint Paul says that a woman in church should have her head covered. The mantilla worn in the church enables the men, who have to stand in the rear of the women, to obtain a view of the altar and see all the service. In this country the women who go to church wear a head gear of such enormous proportions that persons sitting in the back pews cannot obtain a view of the altar unless they stand on stilts. The singing was by male voices, as females were not allowed to sing in the churches of Brazil, nor in Portugal, nor in Spain, for that matter.

We traversed the city and found many strange things. The aqueduct that conveys the water to the city from the springs on the hillsides some fourteen miles from the city, is a massive structure of solid masonry. It looks as though it was built to endure for all time. It is built of stone on a double tier of arches, and the trough is covered with brickwork, which prevents evaporation and also keeps the water comparatively cool. There are several receiving cisterns throughout the city, whence it is distributed by Negro water-carriers, called aquedores, who carry the water in wooden vessels that resemble a butter churn, with bright iron hoops, and hold about five gallons. Thus you will encounter the water-carriers with vessels on their heads, trotting along in all parts of the city. The aqueduct strongly reminded the beholder of the remnants of Roman masonry yet to be found in many parts of Portugal and Spain.

The market is an immense quadrangular building of stone, one very high story in height, containing one wide arched entrance on each of its four sides. It is about twenty feet in depth all around, roofed and divided into shops, which are occupied by small merchants. Inside is an open court, large and entirely paved with granite. In the center of the court is a large fountain which discharges a stream of water that rises some feet into the air and then falls back into the large marble basin, where it evaporates and thereby cools the heated atmosphere. In this square are stone tables resting on granite columns, whereon were displayed the innumerable products of that productive country. Beef, mutton, pork, poultry, fish dripping fresh from the ocean, vegetables of every kind to be found in semi-tropical climates, fruits which to enumerate would require a volume of itself; parrots, parroquetes, singing birds that piped the most delicious liquid notes, and last, but not least, were the slaves, male and female, offered for sale in the open market. Here were offered strong men, robust women and children, for sale the same as donkeys and goats. Some of those offered for sale were not more than four months from their native land—Africa. There they were offered on the altar of mammon—all for glittering gold.

Across the harbor from Rio is Preia Grande, where a slave depot is maintained. There the slave schooners,

which are built in Baltimore for that very purpose, discharge their cargoes of slaves under the cover of darkness and dispose of them to the coffee planters at high prices. The enterprise was dangerous because of the activity of the English cruisers which were sent for the purpose of suppressing the nefarious traffic.

> " From Greenland's icy mountains,
> From India's coral strand;
> Where Afric's sunny fountains
> Roll down their golden sand;
> From many an ancient river,
> From many a palmy plain,
> They call us to deliver
> Their land from error's chain."

England had declared slave-hunting to be piracy, and the penalty was a short shrift and a long rope. While upon this subject I am reminded of a tragic occurrence which took place off the coast of Africa in 1845. While England had a fleet of fast sailing cruisers on the African station to break up the slave trade, she invited the United States to co-operate with her to entirely eradicate the inhuman traffic. The executive department of the United States Government was at that time in the hands of Southern slave-holders and their sympathizers, but as we claimed to be a Christian nation, the invitation could not be wholly ignored. Therefore a man-of-war brig, the "Somers," Commander McKenzie, was ordered to the African station to co-operate with the English cruisers in suppressing the slave-buying traffic. While she was sailing along the coast, exploring for the rendezvous and the barracoons of the slave sellers and slave buyers, a passed midshipman on board the brig, who had been reading bad buccaneering books, conceived the idea of conspiring with some of the crew whom he thought he could influence and executing a well-formed plot, seize the vessel, capture the commander and the officers and make them walk the plank overboard in the regular pirate fashion. After dispatching the officers his plan was to offer all those who joined him a share in the robberies which he contemplated; but if any man refused, then overboard with him to join the captain and his officers. After he obtained the full possession of the brig he intended to cruise around the Canary and the Cape de Verde Islands and cut off the East Indiamen that came around Cape Good Hope, send the crews to Davy Jones' locker, and after appropriating all that the vessels contained of value, set them on fire and let them sink.

He approached one of the petty officers and divulged to him his secret, and in that way they enlisted quite a number of the men in their horrible enterprise. But "God moves in a mysterious way His wonders to perform." One of the men who had been enlisted in the murderous conspiracy became conscience stricken. He went to the executive officer, confessed, and divulged the whole plot. In a spirit of contrition he gave a full account of the details and the time for their execution. The executive officer at once apprised the commander of their danger. Commander McKenzie at once ordered the culprit to be put in irons, and all his confederates into confinement. On the following day a court martial was convened, composed of his brother officers. He was put on trial and found guilty of attempt to commit piracy; penalty, death. Capt. McKenzie being the senior captain on the station, as there was no other man-of-war there, he approved the finding and ordered that the sentence be at once carried into effect. As the situation was fraught with great danger, the safety of the vessel and security of the crew demanded prompt action. Therefore on the day following the past midshipman was hung to the yardarm, a fearful example of perverted talent and a depraved heart. In the meantime every loyal man on board was kept under arms until the tragedy was ended, to prevent the malcontents from breaking out into open revolt. The fate of their leader was held up to his confederates as an example of what they might expect if they manifested any signs of insubordination.

When the "Somers" arrived in Hampton Roads and Commander McKenzie had reported to the Secretary of the Navy, there was a tremendous excitement throughout the country, the people taking sides for or against the action of Commander McKenzie. The young officer had been a member of an influential family, and for that reason there was such a pressure brought to bear upon the President that he caused the Secretary of the Navy to order a court martial for the trial of Commander McKenzie, which attracted much attention. After a thorough investigation the court decided that the safety of the vessel and the crew required both firmness and promptness on the part of Commander McKenzie, therefore his action was justified and approved.

From the very nature of the conditions that surround the captain of a ship at sea his authority on board of ship must be supreme. Such being the case, it is of the utmost importance that the captain should be a sober, intelligent, and cool-headed man, for on these qualities depend the safety of the ship and the lives of every one on board of her.

As Brazil is much nearer to Africa than what Cuba is the slavers can reach this market much easier and dispose of their human chattels at less risk than they can by running the gauntlet of making their way to Cuba, where they realize much higher prices for their slaves. All the local transportation is done by the slaves. This is the most extensive coffee market in the world and the transportation from warehouse to ship is done by slaves. They will form a line of about twenty men, each with a sack of coffee that weighs 120 pounds, on the top of his head, and they will march along in single file for a distance of from a half mile to a mile—from warehouse to ship, without stopping. While on their way they maintain a uniform gait by singing a monotone like "You, you, you! Yah, yah!" So they go through the streets with bare shining bodies with short cotton breeches on them. They seem to be unconcerned, and seem to be happy in their way, thereby verifying the adage of Shakspeare—

"Where ignorance is bliss 'tis folly to be wise."

Most of the houses in Rio are built of unhewn stone and covered on the outside with cement, and colored in light shades. As a general rule the houses are built two stories high, with very high ceilings, on account of the warm weather. The roofs are of red tile, as they are in Portugal; in fact, if a man were to drop down in a balloon into one of the narrow streets in Rio de Janeiro—and the streets are all narrow—he might imagine that he was in Lisbon; with this difference, however, Rio is much cleaner than Lisbon. Perhaps this cleanliness is not so much from choice as it is from necessity, as Rio, being in the tropics, is subject to dreadful fevers during the summer months—from February to May. My companion and myself found ourselves in front of a hotel on which was a sign " Hotel do Lisboa." It was now about three o'clock and we felt ravenously hungry, therefore we entered and sat down at one of the many small tables that were ranged around the side of the room. At the upper end of the room was a small bar; the ceiling was very high, the windows were shaded, and the large room was quite cool. The man behind the bar tinkled a tiny bell and a young fellow came out of a rear room and approached us. I told him that we desired to have something to eat, and, if convenient, would like a chicken and vegetables. He answered that it would be ready in half an hour. I afterwards learned how they prepare chicken for the table in Rio. Each hotel has a large coop in the yard back of the kitchen, in which are placed the chickens as they are brought from the country. When the order is received for fried chicken the fowl is taken from the coop, decapitated, and immersed in hot water and the feathers removed. It is then disjointed, wiped, and, presto! it is in the pan frying. In twenty minutes after the order is received the fighting cock that was lustily crowing defiance to all comers, is placed sizzling on a plate before the guest. That's how it is done in Rio. The reason for this is that in tropical climates where the heat is incessant, whatever creature is killed for human food has to be cooked within a very few hours thereafter or else decomposition sets in, and it at once putrifies. We often hear the saying "salt won't save it," and this is true in tropical climate. The beef that is slaughtered during the night must be eaten the next day.

Our first dinner in Rio consisted of fried chicken, green peas, fried potatoes, salad of lettuce, very superior bread, and a bottle of Madeira wine. After which we had coffee with sweet biscuits. We paid two dollars and fifty cents—making it one dollar and twenty-five cents for each one. The money of Brazil is reckoned by milreis, but we had no difficulty in passing our American coin, without being obliged to go to a money changer. The day having been enjoyed in sight seeing, we all met at the jetty at 6 P. M., and were at once surrounded by the boatmen, who offered to take us on board the ship. I asked how much they would charge, and they answered 1,000 reis. My companions protested at such an excessive price; but when it was explained that it was equal to one dollar of American money they became quite satisfied, and one of them remarked that 1,000 reis was a very small sum with a mighty big name. When we arrived on board we were informed that Capt. Blanchard had taken his family to the hotel Pharoux, where he had engaged quarters, but before he left the ship he had ordered young Brainard to prepare himself and leave the ship for good, as he looked upon him as an intruder. The poor young fellow had packed up such clothes as he had retained from his father's outfit, and had been sent ashore in the quarter boat, while the captain, with his wife and child, had gone ashore in his gig. We were all shocked at hearing what had taken place, for the poor youth had made himself liked by all the passengers. How much money he had we of course knew not, but supposed that he had taken but little from his father's stock, because we expected to go around Cape Horn without calling at any port, and therefore would not have any use for money. Besides the captain and his family, we learned that the French gentlemen and their wives had gone ashore to lodge with their country people while the ship should be in port.

The next morning, when we went ashore, we there found young Brainard waiting for us. He then told us that on the day previous the captain made a second demand for all his father's papers, and upon his refusal to yield them up, had given a peremptory order to the mate to "put that boy ashore." Capt. Blanchard had tried to practice that which the Barons of old knew so well how to do:

"The good old way, the simple plan,
Let him take who has the power,
And let him keep who can."

I consoled him all I could, and volunteered to go to the American Consul with him, who, no doubt, would right all his wrongs. We called upon the Consul, who proved to be a corpulent, inactive man, entirely disinclined to listen to the story of the young fellow, but referred him to his clerk, who proved to be a most repulsive and a most insolent Englishman from the Island of Jamaica. A more forbidding representative of the power and dignity of the American nation I never saw than that fellow who sat in his office in Rio de Janeiro, under the protection of the American flag. I at that time wondered how the Secretary of State could conscientiously recommend to the President men for consuls and even embassadors to protect and advise American citizens when abroad, men that are entirely unfitted by talent or experience. Is it proper that a man who owns a sawmill in Maine and has influence to aid Mr. Morrill from Sagadehoc county or Lincoln county to be elected to Congress, that he should be rewarded by a consular appointment? Not at all. First of all he should be an American in heart and in sentiment. Next he should be a shipping merchant or a captain that is familiar with consular duties. If this is done we will have good consuls. To send a lumbermill politician as consul to an important port like Rio de Janeiro is like setting up a lumber mill on the desert of Sahara. They are both out of place, and therefore of no use. Here was a port where at that very time there were more than thirty American vessels, and still the consular business of them all was attended to by a foreigner. In the darkest days of our republic the great Washington said to his generals at Valley Forge: "To-night put none but Americans on guard." A grand admonition. And to-day the people of these United States should say to the President: Henceforth put none but Americans, in heart and in sentiment, in posts of honor in foreign ports to represent our country. As the Consul's clerk gave neither comfort nor information to the young fellow we were obliged to withdraw without having accomplished anything. On this day we strolled around the city and took observations, as we say at sea. I observed that all the streets had a depression from the sidewalk to the center of the street, which formed the gutter, down which the water ran and conveyed the dirt down to the beach. As the water was continually running, the streets were more cleanly than one would expect.

As I have said, the streets are narrow and the houses two stories high, while the second story has a balcony running the whole length of its frontage, the roof of the house extending over the balcony, thereby protecting it from the scorching rays of the tropical sun. Here many of the ladies would sit at their sewing or crochet work and at the same time converse with their opposite neighbors with as much ease as if they were in the same room, as the quiet of the street was scarcely ever disturbed by a passing vehicle, the porterage being all done by Negro slaves. I noticed that the retail merchants pursued their business on the first floor of the house while their families lived on the second floor, which I considered a most convenient style.

When we returned to the ship at night we sat down to a supper of mutton chops, fried plantains, boiled sweet potatoes and hot biscuits. We also learned that the captain had given orders to the steward not to use any salt beef or pork while in port, as that was to be reserved for use at sea; for all salted beef and pork taken on board at Rio had to be brought from the United States or from England, because it is impossible to cure meat in tropical climates. Meat spoils before it takes the salt.

The following morning being the twenty-third day of December, several of us discussed the propriety of observing Christmas Day in a manner befitting its importance. Seven of us agreed to enjoy a grand Christmas dinner on shore. A young lawyer named Shorb, from Richmond, Virginia, and myself were chosen to engage the dinner. When we arrived at the jetty Shorb and myself sallied out together to find a suitable place where to have our feast. We went to several hotels and told our errand, but we could not settle on a place until we came to the Hotel do Lisboa, where Cluffwater and myself had eaten our first dinner in port. We disclosed our mission to the landlord and he told us that he would serve a dinner for seven persons that should be conformable to the celebration of the nativity of our Lord for the sum of fourteen dollars, and the wine, of which he had a large stock in his cellar, should be so much per bottle, according to kind. I suggested Madeira. He said that wine would be one dollar and fifty cents per bottle. He led us up stairs and showed us a small room about eight by ten

A TALE OF TWO OCEANS. 97

feet in size, which was quite large enough for our purpose. We paid him a five dollar piece in advance as an earnest of our bargain.

After having arranged our business we walked around the city and viewed many of the stores, which, for size and display of goods, did not compare with like places in Philadelphia. Everything about the business places betokened a quiet, easy way of doing business. The streets being narrow, left no room for shade trees, therefore it did not compare with Philadelphia when we left on the fifth of October, when the principal streets were shaded by umbrageous trees, carriages passing to and fro, and many other signs of animated life.

We turned our steps towards the beach and as we approached near the palace we saw coaches approaching the palace yard and soon counted six large stage coaches, such as were daily seen leaving Boston for the outlying towns. These were drawn by four fine horses to each coach. One coach, the last one, had two mounted outriders. This coach was occupied by the Emperor of Brazil, Dom Pedro II, and the Empress. On the box sat the driver and a lackey, and on the rear stood two footmen, all in uniform. As there were neither policemen nor soldiers to interfere, we hastened to the grand entrance to the palace and ranged ourselves in double line at the archway, leaving a wide space between the lines. The coaches were gaily painted in yellow and gold while the horses were richly caparisoned. Out of the five coaches, when the attendants opened the doors, descended a number of gentlemen dressed in plain clothes, a few in uniform, and some in cassocks, who, I supposed, were bishops. These gentlemen formed themselves in a double line after their coaches had been driven away. Last of all the Emperor's coach was opened and I, and I suppose many others, saw a real live Emperor for the first time. After he descended he turned and waited upon his wife, the same as any real gentleman would do. Then he offered the Empress his left arm while in his right he held his chapeau. He was dressed in a green, close-buttoned military coat,

8

black breeches with gold stripes down the legs, and military boots. He did not wear a sword, and only upon his breast he wore a single badge, which was blazing with diamonds. The two royal personages passed between the lines of gentlemen, and as they passed the first two they also followed the royal pair, until all the gentlemen were in the royal train. When the royal couple reached to where I stood I saw before me as fine a looking gentleman as I ever saw in my life. He stood all of six feet or more, was admirably proportioned and looked perfectly grand. The Empress was a short, pleasant-faced blonde, and looked diminutive alongside of her imperial husband. They walked up the grand stairway leading to the grand salon. All the spectators followed, but by the time that I reached the grand chamber every one of the grand cortege had disappeared, having withdrawn to the private part of the palace.

When I withdrew from the precincts of the palace and reflected upon all I had seen I was disappointed beyond measure. Here I had seen the Emperor of a great nation return from his country seat to his palace with his courtiers and retinue; had seen him descend from his coach, escort the Empress to the palace, and all this without the beat of drums or blast of trumpets. By the books which I had read in school I was led to expect that when I saw a real live king I would see a wonderful man in ermine cloak, golden crown on his head and a jeweled scepter in his hand, while every one in view would throw himself upon his knees while the king passed. But here was an emperor, more mighty than a king, who entered his palace without the pomp or circumstance supposed to attend royalty. Even more simple than this I saw in Paris afterwards, when Emperor Louis Napoleon was in the zenith of his glory. Early one Sunday afternoon myself and companion engaged a cabriolet to take us to the Bois de Bologne, so that we might see the old historic mill, the grotto and other curiosities, as well as to pass by the Arc. de Triomphe on our way. As we were passing by the Palace of the Tuilleries we saw a barouche drawn by a fine span of horses, a driver sitting on his perch and a footman standing on the rear, while in the carriage sat a gentleman dressed in plain black suit and silk hat, while beside him sat a lady in a traveling suit devoid of any bright colors. The gates were opened by the concierge and the vehicle came into the street. As it turned in the same direction in which we were going, our driver turned his head and said, sotto voce, "*c'est l'empereur.*" Just then the few persons on the sidewalk raised their hats and cried out, "*Vive l'empereur!*" at which the gentleman raised his hat and the lady made a very gracious bow. The driver afterwards told us that their majesties were on their way to the depot to take a special train for the Bois de Vincennes, where a horse-race was to take place. Now I feel convinced that very much that we learn from school-books we find in after life to have been highly colored and much of it entirely unnatural.

When we returned to the ship that night I related to Mr. Bryson all that I had seen, and he said he had seen the King of Portugal, the King of Belgium and the King of Sweden; "but," said he, "what do they amount to compared with General Jackson, the hero of New Orleans? He was a great soldier and afterwards a good President."

We arranged among the seven of us that each one should take some part in the literary exercises of the Christmas dinner, and to me was assigned that of poet of the occasion, as I had already composed some rhymes during the voyage. For this reason I staid on board all day on the 24th. About ten o'clock Capt. Blanchard came on board, and after having examined what was being done on board of the ship, had sounded the pumps, and ordered his gig to return on shore. As he reached the break of the quarter-deck to go over the gangway he said to the mate in an imperious manner, "Mr. Cranston, keep these landlubbers busy; make them work, for there is not an able seaman amongst the whole lot." As he said this a sailor named Tom Harrold spoke, saying, "Captain, I am an able seaman, and not a job has been put in my hands on this ship that I didn't do in a seamanlike manner." Tom was standing by the after main shrouds, seizing on the sheerpole, and as he said this Capt. Blanchard grabbed him by the bosom of his shirt. No quicker said than done. Tom dropped his work and grasped the captain by his immaculate white vest and beautiful white shirt with his tarry right hand. The captain's face became livid. I think a tiger could not have looked more ferocious. He looked Tom right in the eyes; but Tom's gray eyes never quailed. After a minute the captain, seeing the cool manner and fearless eyes of Tom, loosed his hold, and then Tom dropped his grip. "Go forward, sirrah," hissed the captain. Tom gave him a derisive smile, turned and went forward. Poor Mr. Cranston said not a word, for he was never made for a fighting man, and as to Mr. Bryson, I think his sympathy was with Tom, for he was the best man he had in his watch. The captain then ordered the mate to go to the guard-ship and demand the arrest of the mutinous sailor. The mate jumped into the gig with two men and rowed to the guard-ship, and in fifteen minutes the guard-boat, with six men and an officer with sword by his side, came alongside. The captain received the officer and explained the trouble to him. The officer called up the four marines, and with their short muskets marched forward and arrested poor Tom. They allowed him to take his monkey-jacket and a few plugs of chewing tobacco to solace him in his confinement. After the prisoner had been taken away the captain changed his rumpled shirt and vest and went ashore. After this we all breathed freer and all felt glad to be left to ourselves.

 I devoted the whole day to the composition of my part to be read at our Christmas dinner. In the evening the mate told me that it was probable that there would be a survey held on the ship, and that it was supposed that the ship would be ordered under repairs as she was not in a proper condition to proceed on the voyage. She would have to be taken up to the upper harbor, where the wharves were, discharged and hove down to calk the bottom, as there was no graving dock in Rio. A ship, when she is empty, is easily hove down until her garboard streak is out of the water, and then a floating stage is hauled alongside and the bottom is calked, payed and painted. The mate said this would probably take three months' time. This was a very discouraging outlook, but we had to grin and bear it.

The next morning ushered in Christmas Day. Early in the morning the joyful sounds of bells from the very numerous churches on shore floated over the water in sweet melodious strains and struck upon our ears in sweet, diminished cadence. We felt glad to know that we were in a Christian land. On this day was the Redeemer of mankind born in Bethlehem of Judea. On this day were the humble shepherds on the plains of Judea advised by the heavenly angels of the birth of the Redeemer of mankind.

We arrayed ourselves in our Sunday go-to-meeting best, and after breakfast we went ashore. As we passed the guard-ship we saw poor Tom on deck. He waived his hand in salutation and we all heartily responded. But we felt that we had our hands in the lion's mouth, and dared not interfere in his behalf, for if we incurred the captain's enmity we trembled for the consequences. After landing at the jetty everybody we met was arrayed in gay attire. The large stores were all closed and there were tokens on all sides that it was a grand holiday. At ten o'clock the grand mass was celebrated in all the churches, notably in the Emperor's chapel. Although a large edifice, yet it was not large enough to accommodate all that desired to enter. Nevertheless in a city containing more than fifty churches it was not difficult to gain entrance into one of them.

In the afternoon, as is the usual custom on grand holidays, there was a bull-fight in the amphitheater devoted to such exhibitions. One bull at a time was let into the arena, then the bandalier would approach him with a red cloth or guidon, which he swung before the bull, thereby illustrating the old adage of "shaking a red rag before a mad bull." At this the bull would make a rush at the man and the expert bull-fighter would quickly move to one side and away went the bull with his head down and his tail up, which caused roars of laughter. Then came the spadores with small barbed lances decorated with particolored paper. The lance had a barbed point, which penetrated the hide sufficient for the barb to hold by and nothing more, and whenever the spadore succeeded in darting one into the bull's hide he was applauded to the echo, for be it remembered that the bull wasn't idle while this was going on, and had he caught his tormenter he would perhaps have hurt him some, but the tips of the bull's horns were inclosed in some sort of buffers. There were several bulls brought in one after the other, but no injury was inflicted on man or beast.

Now I will here say that I have read many diatribes written by well meaning humanitarians, all denouncing the practice of bull fights. As to this I have nothing to say in defense of bull fighting for I do not approve of it, but how immeasurably worse is the horrible practice of man fighting. Among these people bull fighting is fostered by the government, and therefore they are to the manor born. But the English speaking people are more highly educated, and as Pope says "'tis education forms the common mind," and for that reason more is expected from the people of the United States. Americans train men to enter the prize ring and fight for a purse of thousands of dollars. Where are our learned, eloquent preachers that they allow such brutal practices without raising their voice in condemnation of such brutal pastimes, so demoralizing to men and so evil teaching to boys? They stand in the pulpit on a Sunday and they turn their mental spyglass towards countries that encourage bull fights and lotteries—which, it must be admitted, are injurious to the morals of the people—but they are a mere bagatelle compared with prize fighting. As our Divine exampler has said: "Thou hypocrite, cast out first the beam out of thine own eye, and then shalt thou see clearly to pull out the mote that is in thy brother's eye.

The American spectators left the Plaza do Toros very much dissatisfied with the performance, because there was neither a bull killed nor a man gored. They said it was too tame.

We had agreed to be at the Hotel do Lisboa at 6 o'clock,

and accordingly we wended our way to that place, where we arrived at half-past six. When we arrived and entered the grand dining-room the landlord greeted us in a very friendly manner, and directed one of the waiters to guide us upstairs to the banquet room. We were escorted up a flight of spiral iron stairs that led up from the rear part of the first floor. Some of my companions asked if we would be obliged to come down the same way. When I asked the waiter he laughed heartily, and told us that the broad stairway led down the front into the street. This explanation satisfied my friends, and we wended our way to the little room that had been prepared for us. Here we found a well prepared table, in the center of which was placed an immense candelabra, holding twelve wax candles, which lighted the room with a soft mellow radiance. There were plates for seven persons, with the usual paraphernalia of a well appointed table. After we were seated the master of ceremonies delivered the following Scotch introductory to the feast:

"Some have meat who canna eat,
Some have na meat to eat it;
But we have meat and we can eat;
So let the Lord be thank it."

Our first dish was prawns—which are a specie of very large shrimps, which are quite common in New Orleans and Mobile as well as in Rio; these had been freed from the shell and seasoned with shallots vinegar and sweet oil. They were fine and supposed to increase the appetite. The next was vegetable soup; then fish—resembling in size the large Labradore herring—these were fried in oil. Then we had two roast chickens stuffed with Italian chestnuts—these were very fine. My companions had never before eaten such a dish, and they were delighted. Then a dish that we asked the waiter the name of. He said it was puchara. It was made of mutton, leeks, peas, carrots, and potatoes, and seasoned with green peppers. It was very piquant and very palatable. Then we had plantains fried in butter. After these substantials had been disposed of and washed down with copious draughts of Madeira wine, the waiter cleared the table and brought dishes of almonds, walnuts, raisins and Brazil nuts, besides some sweet biscuits and more fresh bread, after which the waiter brought seven more bottles of wine, and then withdrew. We were now just entering into the spirit of the occasion. The toast master arose and announced: My friends: "The day we celebrate, Christmas." Drank standing. As by previous arrangement this was responded to by Mr. Shorb, the young Virginia lawyer, as follows:

"My friends, the very name of Christmas brings a flood of recollection to my mind that causes tears of fond remembrance to suffuse my eyes. I can picture in my mind the old plantation in Virginia where I first saw the light of day, the roomy mansion, the large capacious rooms, the ample hearth with the yule log, which was placed therein on Christmas eve. My venerable father in his big chair on one side of the fireplace, and my darling mother in her cushioned rocking-chair on the other side, while we children sat in a semicircle facing the cheerful fire on the hearth, while father told us the stories of olden times of Christmas. When Christmas eve arrived all the field hands on my father's plantation were given a complete exemption from labor, only being required to feed and care for the stock during the holidays, which extended from Christmas eve until the day after New Year's day. The hands were allowed to visit their friends on the neighboring plantations and to receive visitors during the day. In the evening my father would call into the house the fiddler and the banjo player—for there was no plantation in Virginia without its musicians—and they would play and sing old plantation melodies, interspersed with religious Methodist hymns—for the negroes of Virginia are religious and their religion runs into sacred song just as naturally as a mountain rivulet runs into its neighboring creek. During the evening the pitcher of cider was passed around, and occasionally my father would send a servant into the cellar to bring up a bottle of old peach brandy, which was passed among the men in moderate quantities. The Christmas day service at the little country church was more simple than that which we beheld to-day, but none the less sincere, and I trust none the less acceptable to our heavenly Father. For has He not said 'Where two or three meet together and that in my name there will I be in the midst of them.' After the service we would all return home, there would be a table set that would be impossible to describe—turkey, chicken, venison; and, not forgetting the staple Virginia dish, hog and hominy. Thus was celebrated the Christmas in old Virginia, and I here express the hope that all here present may reproduce this picture, some future day, in the bosom of their own family and around their own fireside."

This was followed by the song:

" Carry me back to old Virginia,
To old Virginia's shore."

The next toast: "The President of the United States." Drank standing. This was responded to by a young man named Rockefeller, from Columbia county, New York, as follows:

"My friends, I little thought last Christmas when I participated in the festivities of the season at my father's house in Smoky Hollow, about twelve miles from the city of Hudson, that one year from that time I would be thousands of miles away from my native land, in a country ruled over by an Emperor. But such are the vicissitudes in man's earthly career. The young bird, when he is full fledged, has to leave the parent nest, and by the same rule of nature the boy, when grown, has to leave the parental roof and strike out for himself, and by that rule we are all of us here to-day. I was born but a few miles from Kinderhook, the home of ex-President Van Buren, and often have seen that honored gentleman after he had retired from public life. My father would say to me: 'My boy, when you see Martin Van Buren you are in the presence of a man who, during his presidency, was greater than any potentate on earth, for he was the acknowledged head of a great and powerful nation. He was placed there by the voice of his fellow citizens, who saw in him the qualities of a wise and good ruler, and when the constitutional limit of his rule was reached he withdrew to this, his rural home, to pass his days in quiet contentment among his old neighbors, who look upon him as one of themselves. My boy, this country changes rulers without any convulsion, or war of claimants, as in monarchical countries, for here everything is done according to law under the Constitution.' My friends, this is the first country that I have ever been in that is ruled by a monarch, and I must say that the people seem contented and happy, but I learn from history that every country that is ruled by a monarch may be likened to a beautiful land under which is hidden a burning volcano, that is liable to break out at any moment, scattering death and desolation in its track. As for myself I will here say of my country, in the words of the poet:

> " Where'er I roam, what'er my lot may be,
> My heart untraveled fondly turns to thee."

Song:
> " My country, 'tis of thee,
> Sweet land of liberty,
> Of thee I sing."

The next in order was the poem of the evening which had been assigned me to write. I arose and recited the following lines on wine:

WINE.

> Preachers may preach and teachers teach,
> Of the evil effects of drink;
> Yet 'tis music sweet, to a man of wit,
> To hear the glasses clink.

> There's Webster and Clay—
> Now in their day, this nation's affairs do guide,
> At eleven A. M. each day are seen
> With bottles by their side.

> Say what you will, argue with skill,
> 'Tis true beyond a doubt,
> Sparkling wine is a gift divine,
> Life would be dull without.

My composition was received with great favor, and as they were ready to drink toasts they drank to the poem of the evening.

The evening was advancing apace, and as no boats were allowed to pass around the harbor unchallenged after twelve o'clock, midnight, we prepared to start for the beach. We summoned the waiter and asked for our bill. He soon returned and placed the bill upon the table. Oh! horror! our bill was thirty-five dollars. I thought of the old couplet:

" We laugh loud and gay till the feast is o'er,
But when the bill comes in we laugh no more."

We had made our calculations for the price of the dinner and for seven bottles of wine. But here we were—we had found the wine so seductive that unconsciously we had imbibed double our allotted quantity; therefore our dinner bill, added to what we had expended during the day, exceeded our money on hand. In this quandary we called for another bottle of wine, and told the waiter that we invited the landlord to drink to the El Nataló, with us. The landlord soon appeared, and nothing loth, drank with us. We then explained to him that our bill—with the bottle just consumed added—was thirty-six dollars and fifty cents, and deducting the five dollars which we had paid in advance, left a balance of thirty-one dollars and fifty cents. We told him that we had among us twenty-nine dollars, and that it might take two dollars to pay the boatmen to take us on board the ship; therefore, if he would accept the twenty-seven dollars we would make up the balance by our patronage while we were in port. The good man readily accepted the money, and showed his good will by inviting us to take another bottle of wine with him, which we accepted. We then started for the street by the broad stairway. As we sallied forth from the house and began to breathe the fresh night air the fumes of the wine began to rise into our heads, and some of my companions became quite hilarious. The singing mood came upon them, and they began the then common song:

" We won't go home till morning,
We won't go home till morning,
We won't go home till morning,
Till daylight doth appear."

We found that there were others in the narrow streets celebrating like ourselves, and I began to feel apprehensive of some trouble. However, we reached the jetty after having been admonished by two policemen not to be so noisy. I told them that we were celebrating El Natalô, and were on our way to the ship. When we arrived at the jetty we found only two boats there, and we were obliged to pay out the two dollars which the landlord had allowed us to retain, to take us to the ship. After we had embarked I began to breathe easy, for I had dreaded some trouble, because, as the old adage has it: "When wine is in, wit is out." As we pulled by the guard ship we were challenged, and the boatmen gave the proper response, and we were allowed to proceed. As soon as we had passed the guard ship my companions began to sing, in an uproarious voice, a song that was then in vogue—which had been composed after the battle of New Orleans, where General Jackson, with his untrained American troops but few in number, had defeated General Packenham with his well trained English troops, fresh from victories over the French troops that they had driven from the Peninsular of Portugal and Spain.

The song ran thus:

"One Frenchman whip two Portuguees,
One Englishman he'll whip all three,
One Yankee'll whip all four, you see!
And that's the way we do.

CHORUS.

And that's the way we do,
And that's the way we do,
And that's the way we do,
And play the banjo too.

Their boldness brought to my mind the words of Burns:

"Inspiring John Barleycorn,
What dangers thou dost make us scorn;
With tupenny worth we fear no evil,
With usquebaugh we'll face the devil."

However, as our Portuguese boatman didn't understand a single word of this, therefore their national pride was not wounded. Well, we arrived on board our ship about twelve o'clock, midnight; the man on the anchor watch helped all hands aboard, and after a jolly Christmas day in 1849, we were glad to retire to our berths for the night. When we went ashore the following morning we learned that a brother of young Brainard had arrived in port. I was exceedingly glad to hear this news, for the youth had told me that his brother had sailed from New York in a hermaphrodite brig as second mate, bound to Para, Brazil, and knowing the desolate condition of the young fellow I was glad to hear that a person in interest who had a right to look into the matter had arrived in port. On this I strolled off alone and viewed some of the numerous churches with which Rio abounds. The exterior is not grand, yet they show considerable taste; but for solidity of build they excel anything of the kind in the United States; they looked as if they were built to defy the ravages of time. It was evident to me that the city had been built by a people more active and energetic than those that we met daily—for the native Brazilians are languid and inactive, and not to be compared with their Portuguese progenitors. The city looked to me as though it was completed—that all that ever had been contemplated was finished. I didn't see a house in course of construction nor any new enterprise being carried out. I attributed this to the enervating effects of the tropical climate, for there are no more industrious and plodding people than the inhabitants of old Portugal.

About one o'clock I became hungry, and as the cost of the dinner of the day before had made quite an inroad into my cash, I had to look about as to where I could satisfy my appetite at the smallest cost. As I was passing one of the squares I saw a modest little grocery, in the window of which was a large platter heaping full of fried fish, resembling large herring, and a number of rolls of fresh bread. I stepped inside and asked the attendant how he sold the fish. He looked at me in astonishment, but told me that the price was ten reis apiece—equal to one cent American money. I asked how much per roll for the bread? He said fifty reis—equal to five cents of American money. I bought five fishes and one loaf of bread, and asked permission to stop behind a lot of boxes to eat them. He granted my request, and I ate the fish and the bread and drank a big draught of pure mountain water, and when I had finished my humble repast I felt as well satisfied as if I had feasted on turkey and champagne. After having passed the day in sight-seeing I returned, about five o'clock, to the jetty, when I heard the news of a sad and tragical event.

As I have said before, there was a ship-chandler store facing the harbor, just below the Hotel Pharoux, conducted by an American, and resorted to by all new arrivals to hear the latest news from the United States. Among others, Capt. Blanchard made daily calls at this place. It seems that young Brainard, when he met his brother, had recounted to him the melancholy affair of the serious wound inflicted upon their father, who, for that reason, had to be taken ashore, and how he, by the intervention of the pilot, had been allowed to take his father's place; how the captain had, on the voyage, demanded all the papers that concerned his father's consignment on board the ship, and because he had declined to yield to the captain's unjust demand, he had thrown him ashore among strangers. This account of the misfortune of his dear father and his brother, combined with the fact that he himself had been left in the hospital at Para suffering from tropical fever, excited the young man to such a degree that he became frantic with grief and anger. The day after his arrival in Rio the elder Brainard, accompanied by his younger brother, waited around the ship-chandler's until the captain should make his appearance. About four o'clock in the afternoon the captain strolled into the store, and the lad pointed him out to his brother. Brainard told the captain who he was, and pointed to his brother, who was at the door, to confirm his identity. Capt. Blanchard replied, "that if he had any complaint to make as to the legality of his action he must lay the same before the American consul. But, if he had any personal grievance he could step out of the store and he could right it, there and then." The young man walked from the back part of the long store, followed by the captain. As the young man stepped over the threshhold he turned to face the captain, when the latter drew back his right arm and let fly a terrific blow at Brainard's face. The young man ducked his head just in time to escape the blow that would have laid him "hors de combat." The failure of the captain to reach young Brainard had caused him to waste his strength on the desert air. The momentum of his fist was so great that it caused his body to sway forward, and at that moment young Brainard, in the twinkling of an eye, pulled his sheath knife and plunged it into the breast of the captain. The captain exclaimed, "I am killed!" and fell back into the arms of a person who had hurried from the rear of the store. He was at once taken, by those who gathered around him, and carried most tenderly to his rooms in the hotel, where his grief-stricken wife met him with loud screams of terror. Doctors were at once summoned, who took charge of the wounded man. In the meantime the two brothers stood right still at the scene of the tragedy until the police arrived, to whom they were pointed out, and were at once taken to jail.

It being now after six o'clock, I felt that it would be useless to go to the jail to interview the brothers, therefore I joined my fellow passengers and went on board the ship. At the supper table, at which the chief mate presided, scarcely a word was said about the dreadful affair, all being apprehensive that an expression of opinion might prove prejudical to their own well being; feeling that a very long voyage was yet before us, and not knowing how affairs might turn out, I resolved in my mind that hit or miss I would espouse the cause of the two young fellows, so far as to see that they should secure fair treatment. To apply to the consul I knew would be of no use; as I before said, he was a nonentity. While strolling around the city I had made the acquaintance of a Hollander who had a furniture-making shop where he made chairs, tables, and such like in the front part, and had living rooms for himself and his family in the rear part. I had found him a very friendly man, and he had told me much about the Brazilians and their mode of life. He said they were a simple-minded and kind-hearted people, indolent and confiding, and if a man once won their good will they were his friends through thick and thin. As to himself and his wife, they found no congenial company among the natives, as they differed in their habits of life and in their religion. He and his wife had resolved, when their circumstances would permit, which would be in a short time, to return with their children to their fatherland to spend the evening of their life among the scenes of their childhood. To this good man I resolved to apply in the emergency for advise and guidance. I kept my own counsel and retired to my berth. The next morning I arose, shaved myself, and dressed myself scrupulously neat, and after breakfast I went ashore with my fellow passengers. We went to the hotel and inquired about the captain. We were informed that he was very low, indeed, as the knife had penetrated to very near his heart. The two doctors in attendance had said that it was a most miraculous escape from instant death. They said that if the fresh sea breeze would blow every day, that, with good nursing, might bring him around again; but if the winds went down and the summer heat set in, that would cause fever to supervene, in which event he would have no chance for recovery. Above all things they ordered absolute quiet for the patient, that no one should approach his bed but his wife and attendant. After receiving this news I immediately slipped out by myself and inquired my way to the jail. When I arrived at the somber looking place I approached the iron gate and begged the gatekeeper to allow me to speak to the jailer. He called out to his mate and desired him to call the jailer. In a minute or two the jailer, in his uniform, came to the gate, and the gatekeeper pointed to me, and said something to him. He then approached the iron barricade, and as he did so, I made a profound bow, and when I told him my business there, he directed the gatekeeper to let me in. When I was admitted I at once proceeded to inform him about the affair of the youngest of the two prisoners, and what misfortunes he had suffered from the very first day that the ship had left Philadelphia until the very day of the second tragedy. The recital of my simple story produced such an effect upon him that he at once directed me to follow him.

We ascended a flight of wide stone steps and landed on a wide, well lighted corridor. At the right hand were large iron-barred windows which faced a stone-flagged court. At the left-hand was a large grated door opening into an immense room wherein there appeared to be more than a hundred persons of all colors and nationalities. The jailer directed one of the prisoners to call the two young Americans that had been brought in the evening before. In a few moments I saw young Brainard, in company with another person, making their way towards the grated door. As soon as he saw me the poor youth burst into irrepressible tears, while his companion preserved an air of stolid indifference. I told him how very, very sorry I was to learn of the dreadful occurrence, and that I had come to him to offer my sympathy and my service. He then introduced me to his brother, at the same time saying that the South American fever had left him but a wreck of his former self. And he might well call him a wreck, for he looked so emaciated that he seemed to be nothing more than a cadaver. He appeared to be about twenty-five years of age, with a dull, listless look, and seemed as though he didn't care what became of him. The youth described to me the particulars of the encounter between his brother and the captain; of the latter's brutal and bullying manner, and of his effort to kill his poor, tottering brother with one blow of his powerful fist. But, as to the result, he had no idea in the world that his brother would resort to such extreme measures. But it was now done and could not be recalled. But as to himself he was just as ignorant of his brother's design before the occurrence as a child unborn. I proffered my services in his behalf, and told him that I would proceed to do anything that he wanted done. He replied that he could not do much without money; he had a small sum that he had retained from his father's purse, and his brother had received from the American Consul at Para the three month's wages which the law required of the captain of the vessel when he placed a man in the hospital in a foreign port. And, further, there was the valuable shipment of goods of his father's, which would have to be landed in order to heave the ship down for repairs. I told him I would proceed at once to see what could be done. I at once proceeded to the shop of my new made friend, the Hollander. When I arrived at his house I found him there, working away on some beautiful Brazil wood which he was turning, with a foot-lathe, into highly ornamented chair legs. He greeted me pleasantly, and bade me sit down. I at once opened the object of my call, and told him the story of the youth from the very beginning.

After he had heard me through he said it was a most deplorable affair, and that he felt a hearty sympathy for the two unfortunate strangers. He then told me of a native lawyer, who was of Dutch parentage, named Van Praag, and a man of fine talents and great influence in the community, and he was confident that if he would espouse the cause of the two young men, whatever was possible he would do it for them. He wrote the name and address of the lawyer, and placed his own name at the bottom of the paper.

I at once went to the designated place and the house. I asked the Negro porter for the master, and he directed me up a flight of stairs. When I arrived at the landing I found myself on a balcony overlooking a courtyard that was a veritable Garden of Eden. There were banana and fig trees, rose bushes and magnolias, and in fact almost everything to delight the senses. This on the right hand side. On the left were the doors for entering the house. I told the footman my business, and at the same time handed him the paper which I had received from my friend Vanderdekken. He opened the door into a room that fronted on the street and bade me enter, which I did. I found myself in a room that was not very large, and lined on all sides with bookcases which were filled with enough books to start a large New England library. In the center was a large table covered with green baize on which were a few books, some of which were open, inkstand, pens and blank paper. I now knew I was in the office of the lawyer and felt convinced that it was his family mansion. I stood in the room for more than five minutes anxiously waiting for the man that might help my young friends.

After a time the gentleman came with the scrap of paper in his hand and bowed to me and bid me good morning. If I had not been told who he was I would have supposed that he had just landed from a Dutch ship. He was a broad faced, light complexioned, curly headed, blue eyed man of about forty years of age. His genial manner caused me to feel quite free to tell him my story, which I proceeded to do in as few words as possible. After I had finished my narrative he asked me as to their means at hand. I told him of the limited amount they had, but that they had a large quantity of valuable freight on board the ship, which would have to be discharged in order to repair the ship, and then it might be got hold of or be hypothecated to whoever would advance the necessary money to defray expenses that have to be incurred. He placed his left elbow upon the table and rested his forehead upon his left hand. He remained in meditation for as much as three or four minutes, apparently unconscious of my presence. After a time he raised his head and said: "Young man, if I find that everything is as you have related I shall take this case in hand and I will try my best to help the two poor strangers." He looked up at the clock and said, "It is now eleven o'clock; you may come here at half-past two o'clock, and I will then be ready to go with you to the jail where I can see the two young men." I withdrew from his presence with a light heart, for I felt that I had enlisted the sympathies of a powerful friend in the cause of the two captives.

As I walked along the street I saw a sight that reminded me of Gibraltar. That was a goatherder driving a number of goats from house to house, and at each house where he stopped he would take an earthen measure from a girdle around his waist and proceed to draw from the udder of one of the goats as much milk as was desired to supply his customer. After this he would secure the measure to his girdle and trot along again to the house of the next customer. He would call out to the goats in a way that sounded like "rah-bah-rarm," and the goats would run along and halt directly in front of his next customer. I thought if this mode prevailed in Philadelphia that the Fairmount Waterworks would have the demand upon its aqueous supply very much diminished.

I strolled around until I became hungry, and finding an humble posada or inn I went in and asked for a cup of coffee. It was brought to me and also a small roll of bread. The coffee was delicious, flavored with goats' milk and sweetened with loaf sugar. I asked the lady how much, and she answered fifty reis; this was equal to five cents of American money, which I paid.

As I passed into the street it impressed me with its quietness; not a vehicle nor scarcely any person in the street; profound stillness with only the occasional salutations of the women to one another from opposite balconies. I wondered to myself, when do these people work and how do they earn their living?

At two o'clock I wended my way back to the mansion of the lawyer. When I arrived there the Negro porter recognized me and waived his hand for me to enter and ascend the stairs, which I did. When I reached the landing the footman went to the door of the office and announced me to his master. As he returned to the door he waived to me to enter. When I went in the lawyer was seated at the table examining and poring over some books. When I entered he bade me sit down and said that he would go with me directly. He withdrew into the interior portion of the mansion, from whence I heard childish voices and innocent laughter, giving proof that he was a gentleman of domestic responsibilities. When he returned into the office I saw that he was metamorphosed into a most elegant looking gentleman. He was dressed in white shirt with ruffled bosom, white linen trowsers, white necktie, white Marseilles vest, black alpaca coat, leghorn straw high hat, low morocco shoes and white stockings. In his hand he carried a silk umbrella, which he opened when we reached the street to protect himself from the hot midsummer sun.

When we reached the street he desired me to tell him the story again about the young men, which I did in as few words as possible: How when the steamer towed the ship down the Delaware river the ship was anchored off abreast of New Castle, where we went ashore and brought off several demijohns of whisky; how Capt. Brainard and one other passenger, who had been a volunteer and served under General Scott in Mexico, and for these reasons espoused his cause, while Capt. Brainard, on his side, advocated General Taylor, which culminated in the ex-volunteer cutting the throat of Capt. Brainard. That Brainard being at the point of death was taken ashore, and his young son was allowed to take his father's papers and continue in the ship in place of his father. How the captain had driven him on shore, where his brother, having arrived from Para, had met him, and in an altercation with Capt. Blanchard he had stabbed him and the captain was supposed to be in extreme danger. He then delivered a homily on American jurisprudence, with which subject he seemed to be quite familiar, and said that the laws of the United States, as laid down in the books, were most admirable, but there was a laxity in their enforcement. For example, if such a tragic affair had taken place in the harbor of Rio Janeiro as what had taken place in the Delaware river, the ship would not have been allowed to proceed on her voyage until the witnesses had given their deposition and everything had been done to secure the trial and conviction of the culprit. Further, he said that he had read many decisions rendered by judges in the State law courts of the United States that were so contrary to reason and common sense, on which all laws should be founded, that it led him to the conclusion that many of the judges laid themselves liable to the charge of venality in the discharge of their important duties.

We had now arrived at the portal of the jail. As soon

as the guard at the gate espied the lawyer he spoke to his assistant and he fetched the jailer. The iron gate was at once thrown open and the lawyer was received with much obsequiousness, and after a few words with the jailer was escorted up the stone stairway to the floor above. The lawyer bade me follow. As soon as we arrived at the landing the jailer promptly drew a key from his pocket and opened the iron barred door, and ordered the youth Brainard to come into the corridor. I introduced him to the lawyer, and he then told his plain, unvarnished story, to which the lawyer paid close attention. At the conclusion the lawyer asked about the papers, and the youth told him that he had them secured about his person. The lawyer bid him to hand them over to him, for which he would give him a receipt, which he at once wrote at the desk in the corridor, and then told him to wait patiently until the next day, while he would call upon the magistrate and see what the charge was against him. The youth was then returned inside the grated door and the key turned upon him.

After we returned to the street the lawyer told me to come to his office the next morning at ten o'clock, and he would then tell me what could be done. We now parted and I proceeded to the jetty, it being five o'clock, and having accomplished the engaging of a great lawyer for the two unfortunates, I returned to the ship with a light heart. On board the ship I didn't disclose my doings to any one, as the subject was not one that could be openly discussed. After supper I retired to my berth thoroughly tired with the day's labors, and slept until morning.

The next morning after breakfast I polished myself up and was ready for the first boat, which left the ship at nine o'clock. Many of the passengers, who had money, having found out that they could board ashore in an humble way very cheap, had taken board and lodgings on shore, so that the few impecunious ones like myself felt like interlopers, but for all that we knew that we had a right to be on board, as we had paid our two hundred dollars in Philadelphia to be taken to San Francisco. When we arrived on shore I went immediately to my good friend Vanderdekken and reported progress. He said he was very glad that so accomplished a lawyer as Van Praag had consented to take the case of the two prisoners in hand, and he thought that of itself would go a long ways to ameliorate their condition in the jail, as the lawyer was a man of great influence in the community.

I then went to the office of the lawyer and he received me in his office. He told me that he had obtained an interview with the committing magistrate, on the evening previous, in behalf of the youth, and had explained to him that the crime was committed by the elder brother without the youth's previous knowledge as to what was to take place. Therefore the judge had said that he would give him an answer on this day at three o'clock. The lawyer told me that this was the summer vacation of the courts, lasting from Christmas week until after Saint Sebastian's day, the patron saint of Rio Janeiro, as the harbor was discovered on his anniversary. So he told me to return to his office at two o'clock, at which time I should go with him to the mansion of the magistrate. I withdrew expressing my sincere thanks for his kindness.

As I walked about the city I came upon a large two-story stone mansion surrounded with very high stone walls, above which I could see the tops of trees. It inclosed a large space. I inquired as to the identity of the establishment and was informed that it was an asylum for female children, and that it was under the immediate patronage of the Emperor and Empress, and in charge of an order of religious ladies. There were received female children that were orphans or abandoned by their cruel parents. They were reared and educated in mental and physical usefulness—reading, writing, arithmetic, sewing, cooking, and all useful branches of every day life work. Many young men go there to seek a wife, and when they furnish a guarantee of good moral and industrious character they are allowed into the reception room, where they may meet such young women as are eligible for the duties of wedded life. When they choose one and the desire is reciprocal the young man is required to make a reasonable donation to the institution, or else to furnish a guarantee to do so at a reasonable period in the near future. Such of the girls as are placed with respectable families are looked after by accredited agents of the institution, so that it is said that there is not a little girl within the limits of Rio Janeiro that needs a parent's care but what she receives it with parental solicitude.

I to-day revisited the little grocery facing the square and ate my simple repast of fried fish with the roll of bread, which I paid ten cents for. At two o'clock I presented myself at the office of the lawyer and found him ready to go to the house of the magistrate. As we went along he asked about myself, and I told him I was a sailor, without any domestic ties, and seeking my fortune wherever I thought it could be found. He replied that the best way for a young man to seek fortune was to have industrious hands and an honest purpose, which, in time, will win him a competency and a clean and easy conscience wherewith to enjoy it.

We had now arrived at the place of our destination. In the archway stood a Negro concierge dressed in a livery. He knew the lawyer and bowed profoundly. The lawyer, as we walked into the courtyard, bade him to announce his presence to the magistrate, which he at once went to do, while we seated ourselves on the settees placed around. The lackey soon returned and told the lawyer that his master was ready to receive him. The lawyer arose and proceeded to the door whence the Negro had emerged, and left me seated.

I now reflected over the sad affair of the stabbing of the captain, and how dreadful was the situation of the two brothers, who were now in prison in a strange land, without a relative or a near friend with the power to aid them, for however willing I might be, I was without money and therefore without the means that are indispensable in all emergencies that arise in civilized communities whereby any effective action can be taken.

At the expiration of about fifteen minutes a footman came

to me and told me to follow him. I obeyed and we entered a spacious room with high ceiling and rich stucco work around. The floor was of polished wood, and a number of large heavy chairs with leather cushions were ranged around the room. On a raised dais was an imposing, dark complexioned gentleman, with a large polished wood desk in front of him, and from the wall back of him extended a canopy of rich damask cloth. Over his head was the imperial coat of arms of Brazil. At a table in front of the desk sat a young, pale-faced man, writing a document. The lawyer, who was sitting near the table, motioned to me to approach and I did so with awe, feeling that I was now in the presence of a personage who possessed great power. The lawyer spoke in a familiar manner to the gentleman that sat on the chair of state, and they exchanged a few words. Then the young man passed up the document, which the gentleman read and to which he affixed his name and handed back to the young man, who then folded it and affixed some words to the back and handed the document to the lawyer, who at once, without looking into it, handed it to me, at the same time saying, "Take this to the jail and deliver it to the chief jailer, and he will at once release your young friend, and to-morrow morning you must escort him to my office, and we will then have a conference."

I received the precious document with a throbbing heart. I have my doubts whether General Scott felt more proud of his achievement when he received the surrender of the City of Mexico than I did of mine, through the kind and generous and God-inspired act of this blessed, whole-souled stranger, the lawyer of Rio de Janeiro. I withdrew after giving vent to a profusion of thanks, and as I reached the street I felt so light that I seemed to fly, on the wings of the wind, towards the jail.

When I reached the iron-grated door the gatekeeper sent for the jailer, while I waited on the outside. In a few moments the jailer arrived, and ordered the gate to be opened. As I entered the courtyard I handed the precious document to the jailer, who opened it, read it carefully, folded it and took it to his office, in the rear part of the yard, and returned.

He then told me to sit down on a bench, and ordered one of his attendants to go upstairs with him. While they were gone I looked around me, and observed that the lower or first floor was divided into cells, with strong, heavy doors, and I learned that prisoners, after conviction and sentence, were placed in these cells preparatory to being sent to the stone quarries, some miles away, near the mouth of the harbor. After some ten minutes the jailer and his attendant descended the stone stairs with the liberated young fellow walking between them; as soon as he saw me he ran to me and grasped my hand with intense fervor. He said that words were inadequate to express his feelings, but his action in the future would give proof of his gratitude. As we were in the act of leaving the jailyard, what was my astonishment to see at the gate the chief mate of the ship, Mr. Cranston, with his gold-bowed spectacles on his nose and a broad smile on his face. He grasped young Brainard by the hand and congratulated him on his liberation. I felt perfectly disgusted with such manifest duplicity. But his early arrival at the jail convinced me that the magistrate had sent a doctor to the hotel to learn the condition of the captain before he would set young Brainard free, and that was how the mate got an inkling of what was going on.

After the mate parted from us, I took the youth to the house of my adviser, Mr. Vandardekken, to whom I introduced him, at the same time making due acknowledgment for his great kindness and guidance.

I then accompanied my young friend to the door of his boarding house; after arranging to meet him in the morning, I proceeded to the jetty and took a boat for the ship. I arrived on board at half-past six o'clock and found that the news had preceded me. My fellow-passengers said I had done a good deed; but, said they, how will you stand with the captain if he gets well and takes charge of the ship? This set me to thinking; and I discovered that I had become a marked man on board. I was a little late—as six o'clock was the hour for supper—but the steward served me an extra-fine supper, and impressed upon me that I had acted the part of a good Samaritan, and to have no fear of the consequences, where a noble act was concerned. I learned that during the day the steamship "Tennessee" had arrived—twenty-six days from New York—and therefore, as this was the twelfth day of January, she would have papers as late as December 17th, 1849. I determined to go on board of her the following day and obtain some New York papers which had been read and were of no further use to the people on board. I retired to my berth with the feeling of having done what was right, but I could see by the manner of the mate that I would be in bad favor after this episode.

The next morning, as I was preparing to go ashore, Mr. Bryson, the second mate, spoke to me, and said: "Young feller, I hear that you made yourself busy enough to get young Brainard out of the jug. You done a good deed. I feel for the two young fellers, although I never saw tother one, but they are both Philadelphia boys, and so'm I, and that's enough for me. Now, I'll give you a piece of advice, and that is this—don't you have anything more to do with the old man than you can help. When we leave here, don't you turn to work again or have anything to do about deck—eat, drink, and sleep, the same as any passenger, and then if the old man interferes with you it will be a sorry day for him. He is my commanding officer and I don't want to say any more. Keep clear of the mate, for he and the captain suck through the same quill." After this kindly admonition he turned to attend to his usual duties, while I jumped into the boat, with others of my fellow-passengers, and we went on shore.

After landing I went to my young friend and found him already to proceed to the lawyer, which we did at once. When we arrived at the house the porter bade us go upstairs, and when we ascended to the balcony the footman escorted us to the office, where we found the lawyer awaiting us. He saluted us pleasantly and congratulated Brainard on having obtained his freedom. On the table I saw that he had the bills of lading, the list of goods, and many of the bills of goods which were receipted. "Now," said the lawyer, "we will enter into business at once. I see that your father has goods on board the ship 'Samson' that cost him all of two thousand dollars. A marine board has surveyed the ship and have ordered her to be discharged, and repaired so as to be seaworthy. Now, the question is whether enough of these goods can be segregated from the cargo, and sold here, to enable you to defray the necessary expenses that you will have to incur in order to employ counsel to defend your brother in the court. For you must know that in Brazil you cannot buy justice—which I fear is not the case in your country—but you can make a proper presentation of your case, with all the mitigating circumstances in favor of the accused, and to do this, involves much labor and legal skill; and here, as in other countries, such services must be paid; for, as the holy writ tells us, 'the laborer is worthy of his hire.' I will now go to the American Consul, with whom I am well acquainted, and will see what can be done. And if I fail to make any satisfactory arrangement with him, I will then draw up a bond of hypothecation which you and your brother will sign and acknowledge in the presence of the American Consul, and I will send that to San Francisco and there it will be collected when the 'Samson' arrives there. This being disposed of for the present, I will advise you as to your brother. When I saw him in the prison my heart softened to see a living skeleton as he is, standing there charged with such a heinous crime as an attempt at murder. And, on the other hand, he must be a cowardly bully that would raise his hand to strike such a shadow of a man as your brother is. Now let me advise you, as I am given to understand that you and brother have some money between you, the very first act of yours should be to arrange with the nearest eating place to the prison to supply you with good and regular meals for your brother, which you must take to him yourself, and I will arrange with the jailer that he shall allow the prisoner to come out into the corridor to eat his food. Tell him to eat and become strong, and as to the rest he may trust to me, with unwavering confidence, that all will be done for him that legal skill and acumen can accomplish.

"Now as to your good friend here, he has proved the truth of the old adage, which says:

"A friend in need is a friend indeed,
And prized as such should be, sirs,
While summer friends, when summer ends,
Are off and o'er the sea, sirs."

"Now that he has served you so well you had better release him from any further attendance for fear that it may excite a prejudice on the part of the captain against him." He then bade me good by, adding that he thought I was an honest fellow and hoped I would succeed in life. I never saw him after that time; but whenever I met a good man my mind always reverted to the good lawyer in Rio de Janeiro. After we withdrew from the lawyer young Brainard went to the jail to see his brother and select a place from which to obtain his meals, while I strolled towards the harbor, and on the way stopped again at the little tavern where I again took a cup of rich coffee with goat's milk and a nice roll, for all of which I paid five cents, for now "grass was getting short with me."

When I reached the beach I found several California bound passengers who, like myself, desired to visit the steamship "Tennessee," and we at once engaged a boat to take us out and back for two dollars, as she laid all of three miles from the shore, for the harbor of Rio is at least ten miles wide in front of the city. We were six in number, each one paying his proportion. As we were going off to the steamer some of them said that if they could secure a passage on her they would gladly forfeit what they had paid for their passage on the "wind jammer" and go in a craft that could sail right in the wind's eye. But alas, for their hopes! When we arrived on board we were received in a most friendly manner. The purser informed the applicants for a passage that it had been arranged in New York to have as many passengers on the Isthmus by the time that the steamer arrived in Panama as the ship could accommodate; therefore they had been ordered, before leaving New York, not to take any passengers on board at Rio, where they were to touch to replenish their stock of coal. As to obtaining newspapers we were more fortunate. The chief engineer was named Mr. Bills—who afterwards established a shop on Jackson street in San Francisco, to repair the machinery of steamboats—he kindly instructed one of the stewards to gather up all the stray papers that he could find and give the same to us. We therefore had a heterogeneous collection of newspapers from all the prominent cities in the eastern and middle States, in date up to December sixteenth previous. To us this was a grand feast. In these we found the news that made me feel very uneasy, for it announced the fact the California fever was increasing in every town from Eastport to the Capes of Virginia. Mechanics were leaving their workshops, small farmers were mortgaging their farms, and even ministers were leaving their pulpits to join the grand procession that was marching towards the El Dorado. I felt as though we were left out in the cold. I thought that by the time we arrived there that every bushel of gold dust in California would be dug up, sacked, and carried away. These thoughts seem ridiculous at this late day, but it must be borne in mind that at the time when we started for California we had only a crude idea about the manner of getting the gold, or as to how much we would dig up per day. In fact, all we did know was that there was lots of gold in California, and that we only knew by hearsay.

I found in a Philadelphia paper an article that interested me very much. It was nothing less than the account of the trial of the culprit that cut the throat of Capt. Brainard on October fifth, on board the ship "Samson," then lying off New Castle and bound to California. The article detailed all the particulars of the tragic affair; how Capt. Brainard was taken ashore, supposed to be in a dying condition; how the culprit was brought ashore at the same time and imprisoned; how the captain hovered between life and death for many days; how by skillful medical treatment and careful nursing by his family, who attended him in New Castle, he had finally recovered; how the culprit was put on trial and was acquitted by reason of there being only one witness to testify against him, and thus he had escaped scot free. I was highly delighted to learn of the recovery of Capt. Brainard, and was resolved to convey the news and the paper to young Brainard the next morning. Every one on board the ship was highly pleased to hear of the recovery of Capt. Brainard, at the same time expressing the hope that Capt. Blanchard would be as fortunate, so that the ship might be quickly put in trim, so that we could resume our voyage towards the land of gold.

The next morning I carried the newspaper ashore with me, and as soon as young Brainard read the account of his father's complete recovery, he became so much elated that he skipped around like one that was demented. I gave him the newspaper that he might show it to his brother, and as I had nothing more to do I sauntered around the town viewing the strange sights. Some of my fellow-passengers forced me, against my will, to go with them to see about buying some crude diamonds, of which they had read in their schoolbooks, wherein Brazil was described as the great depository of the finest diamonds, which were taken out of dark, deep mines in the mountains by slaves. In order to please them, as I couldn't buy a diamond even if they were selling at a dollar a pound, I guided them to the Rua do Ouvidor, which was the center of the rich retail trade. There were four of us, and as we entered the store one of the clerks came forward and I explained our business to him. He at once went to the office in the further end of the store, which, being on a corner, the office faced another and narrower street, and informed the head man. He came forward to where we were waiting and bowed very politely, and I explained to him that my companions were moneyed gentlemen and desired to invest some of their money in crude Brazilian diamonds. As soon as he understood what I had said he burst into an uncontrollable fit of laughter that caused me to feel very much abashed. When he discovered my apparent discomfiture he apologized for his seeming rudeness, and then proceeded to explain that he was a native of Brazil, although he had served his apprenticeship in Paris, but in all his life had only seen as many natural rough diamonds as he could count on his fingers. He said that the government was very strict in regulating the product of the diamond mines and required of the managers thereof a quarterly account of all diamonds obtained, and also demanded a royalty for every diamond that was mined. Then there was an export duty to be paid before they were allowed to be sent abroad. He said the diamond cutting industry was unknown in Brazil; that there were lapidaries in the city, but he didn't know any one of them that cut and polished diamonds. Then he told me that a number of Americans had called at his place on the same errand. I then told him that the Americans imbibe their ideas about diamonds from school-books, in which are published a lot of trash about kings, emperors, diamonds and other things that have no foundation in fact. When I explained this to my friends they seemed much disappointed, having anticipated a large gain from the purchase of diamonds in their natural state.

Our captain was improving daily, as we learned from the mate, as none of the passengers had been allowed to see him.

It was now the eighteenth of January, and yet the ship had not been taken to the upper harbor, where she was to be discharged and hove down for repairs. I felt that we were wasting precious time, and besides I felt uneasy as to how I would get along with the captain after we got to sea. Several of our passengers, among them two gentlemen and their wives, had become disgusted with the ship and had taken passage in another vessel and had already sailed for California. The following day, as I was walking around near the landing, I was surprised to see, among a group of Americans who were passing by, a young man named Simon Brownnell, with whom I had been well acquainted in Boston. I saluted him and as soon as he recognized me he returned the salutation in a most hearty manner. After exchanging the account of our experiences since we had met in Boston, I proceeded and told him how I had taken cabin passage in the ship "Samson," Capt. Blanchard, from Philadelphia for San Francisco, and all other particulars with which the reader is already acquainted. He told me that he was a passenger on board the ship "Urania," Capt. Buckland, from Boston and bound to San Francisco. He told me that Capt. Buckland was of Cape Cod and a most elegant gentleman. I told him that I felt that I was wasting time, and sincerely wished to get on board of some ship where I could work my passage, as I had invested what money I had in Philadelphia in a venture of such articles as I thought I could sell in the land of gold, and the goods were on board the "Samson." He replied that he would introduce me to Capt. Buckland and would recommend me as being a sailor as he knew me to be. I thanked him for his friendly offer and kind intentions. He told me to be at the American ship chandlery at nine o'clock the next morning and he would speak to the captain for me in advance. I again thanked him and promised to be on hand the next morning and then we parted. I was now full of hope. I felt that I saw an avenue of escape from a most disagreeable position. I went on board the ship that evening buoyed by the hope that I would yet escape from the thraldom in which I found myself. I ate my supper and retired to my berth without saying anything to any of my fellow-passengers about my project.

The following morning I divulged my intention to Mr. Bryson, the second mate, whom I looked upon as my friend. He advised me to do so by all means, for he felt convinced that when Capt. Blanchard returned to the ship he would make matters very unpleasant for me, as he looked upon him as being a very vindictive man. I went ashore and reached the American chandlery by half-past nine o'clock. Mr. Brownnell was already there, and after salutations told me that he had already communicated to Capt. Buckland all about me, and he felt confident that I would be given a chance to work for my passage. He requested me to wait with him until the captain came, as he expected him at the chandlery very soon. I waited with my friend and told him many incidents that occurred during my voyage. I told him about Neptune and about the water-spout and other things. While I was rattling with my yarns he admonished me that the captain was approaching. As he indicated I looked up and saw a gentleman approaching that stood at least six feet two inches high, with a Websterian head and brown complexion and the carriage of an admiral. He saluted Mr. Brownnell and Mr. Brownnell introduced me as the person of whom he had spoken the evening before. The captain saluted me with condescension, and I then recited to him my affairs and told him of the dilemma in which I was placed without the means to help myself. After he heard me he said that, although he had a good crew, that some of them were not so expert aloft as men that had always sailed in square-rigged vessels, and therefore, as I was recommended by Mr. Brownnell, he would take me, but did not want to ship me in a formal manner through the consular office as that involved considerable expense, but as he intended to sail on Tuesday or Wednesday I could come on board and bring my chest and he would instruct the mate to permit me to come on board the ship. The captain then left me and passed into the ship chandlery. My heart beat fast at this announcement, and the following beautiful lines came to my mind:

"Ye fearful saints fresh courage take;
The clouds you so much dread
Are big with mercy and will break
In blessings on your head."

For whereas I had been despondent and fearful before, I now felt that the clouds of darkness were breaking away and the bow of promise showed itself to my mind.

I now laid out my plans. I went to the entrance of the Hotel Pharoux and there awaited the arrival of the first mate, Mr. Cranston, who I knew came there daily to make his report to the captain. He arrived about eleven o'clock, and I accosted him in my politest manner. I told him that I had already expended all my spare change, and for that reason would be obliged to stay on board the ship altogether, and now having met an acquaintance he had kindly induced the captain of the ship on which he was a passenger to give me the chance to work for my passage to San Francisco. Now what I desired of him was to secure me an interview with Capt. Blanchard about the balance of my passage money and an allowance of my two months' wages. The mate bade me wait in front of the hotel for a time, and if he found the captain in a condition to converse he would then come down and call me. He went upstairs and I awaited his return, but whatever his answer might be, I had already determined to avail myself of the glorious opportunity to secure a quick passage to California. After fifteen minutes Mr. Cranston came downstairs and told me to follow him. We went upstairs and passed along a wide corridor until we came to the end room, when he opened a door on the righthand side and escorted me into a fine large room with windows opening into the square that looked towards one of the large fountains, which was in full play. Facing the door was the side of a large, high bed, on which reclined Capt. Blanchard, whom I had not seen since the terrible day on which he received his wound. Near the head of the bed sat his wife, and as I entered the captain turned his head and looked at me, and his wife gazed at me with a look of reproach that caused me to feel like a guilty wretch.

The mate withdrew and then the captain said to me in a severe tone, "What do you want?" I then explained that I had an opportunity to work my passage to San Francisco, and I had waited upon him to ask him to make me some concession for the balance of my passage money, and also to pay my wages for the two months' service. He answered severely, "You paid your passage to be taken to San Francisco, and so did all the other passengers. Now I understand that several of them have taken passage from here in other vessels, and have already gone. Yet you are the only one that has approached me to ask me to refund a portion of the passage money. I will not refund you one dollar, for you are not entitled to it. There is the ship; you can stay on her until she reaches her destination, but if you want to leave her I can't prevent you. As to your wages, I will prove to you that I am an honorable gentleman; I will give you my promissory note for the sixty dollars of your wages, made payable when the ship arrives in San Francisco." As this was Hobson's choice, " take that or get nothing," I accepted his offer. He desired his wife to draw up the note at his dictation, and he touched the pen when she signed his name. Then the lady handed it to me. I received it with an humble bow.

When I looked at him and saw his pale, wan face and languid appearance, I wondered to myself how a man of robust build and combative tendencies like him—one that had been the terror of sailors on board of ship—could, after all his triumphs, be brought so low by the hand of a shadow of a man who had just risen from a bed of an almost fatal tropical fever. Surely how true the old adage which says:

" The mills of the gods grind slowly,
But they grind exceeding fine."

I quickly withdrew with a prayer in my heart that I might never meet the like of him again, and, thank God, I never have. I now hurried to the jetty and hired a boat and went on board the ship to take away my chest. Here another surprise awaited me. The sailor Tom, who had been a prisoner on the guard-ship, had just been returned by the same boat that took him away, and a bill had been placed in the hands of the second mate that demanded payment for his detention and board, which would have to be paid before the ship would be allowed to leave port. I told Mr. Bryson that I had come to take my baggage and also to take leave of all hands on board. He congratulated me and said I was acting wisely and wished me a quick and safe voyage to the land of gold. As I was about to leave the ship Tom came to me and asked me to let him go ashore with me in the boat, as he was fully determined to never sail another mile in that ship. I told him I would be only too glad to accommodate him if he could arrange matters with Mr. Bryson, who was in charge of the ship. He told Mr. Bryson that he had served just four months from the first day he came on board in Philadelphia, and had been paid one month's wages the day before we left, and therefore he had three months' wages due to him which he would donate to the captain wherewith to buy more rum, but as to continuing in the ship, he would not do it even if he was offered "a farm down east" at the end of the voyage. As Mr. Bryson could not enforce his authority, Tom bundled his bag and mattress into the boat, and taking a kindly leave of every man on board, we left the ship "Samson," never to set foot on her again.

We reached the shore and engaged two Negroes to help us to take our baggage to the nearest sailor boarding house. We were directed to a house one street removed from the beach, to which place we took our baggage. It was kept by a Frenchman, who was a broad-shouldered, good-natured looking man. When we entered we found the front room to be the eating room and bar. On one side were four small tables; on the opposite side was the bar. He directed us to put our baggage in the next room back, which we found was arranged on one side with berths, the same as on board of a ship, while on the opposite side was piled the boarders' baggage; the room back of this was the kitchen. It was now four o'clock, and the landlord told us that the dinner would be served from six until seven o'clock—so that, as we had two hours in which to look around, we sallied out. As we reached the street Tom opened his mind to me thus: "I'll tell you what I want to do; I want to get a chance to work my passage to California on the same ship that you have secured a berth in, and I want you to show the captain to me when he comes to the beach to go aboard, and I'll do the rest." Well, as this was a reasonable request I yielded, and we walked down towards the jetty and we ensconced ourselves where Tom could not be seen, and there watched for the gig of the "Urania."

About half-past five o'clock I descried the tall, heavy form of Capt. Buckland approaching the landing. He was accompanied by a lady, who I afterwards learned was his wife, and a tall youth who was his son. Tom urged me to approach the captain, and in order to help him I stepped forward in his company. We saluted the captain by doffing our hats and bidding him good afternoon. The captain recognized me, and I then introduced Tom to him. Tom then began with the persuasive eloquence that comes naturally to the people of his country, and told Capt. Buckland that having been in a disagreeable discussion with the captain of the ship in which he arrived, that he had voluntarily left her, and now would like to obtain the chance to work for his passage to San Francisco on the "Urania." Capt. Buckland answered my friend: "I have already engaged to give this man a passage," pointing to me, "and I don't think I can make room for another." "Well, captain," said Tom, "if you'll give me a chance, sir, you'll find that I am an able seaman, and I'll give ready and willing service during the voyage and when the ship arrives in San Francisco I'll stay by her and work until every ton of cargo is out of her." "Well," replied Capt. Buckland, "since you are so liberal with the offer of your service I will confer with my mate to-night and I'll give you my answer to-morrow morning when I come ashore." Tom thanked him profusely, and we withdrew, and the captain entered his gig and was pulled off. I complimented Tom for his persuasive eloquence and predicted that his effort would be successful.

We now returned to the boarding house and seated ourselves at one of the little tables to eat our dinner. It consisted of pottage au legume, a well-seasoned ragout, a salad, good bread, a bottle of indifferent claret, and a cup of rich coffee. While we were eating Tom recounted his experience on board the guardship. He said for breakfast he was given a large pannican of good coffee sweetened with brown sugar, and a loaf of bread. For dinner they gave him a tin dish of stew, made of South American jerk-beef, potatoes, carrots and peppers, a loaf of bread, and a pannican of coffee. During the day he was allowed the freedom of the deck, but within certain limits. At night he, with other sailor prisoners, was locked in the hold of the guardship and gratings put over the hatchways. When the first Friday of his confinement arrived and he declined to eat meat at dinner, the guard was so impressed by his conduct that he quickly brought him a fine dish of fresh fish from his own mess-table. Other sailors that were brought on board from time to time were taken on shore or discharged in a day or so, but he was detained longer than any one else, and all severity was relaxed in his case. He understood that the ship is held responsible for the cost of maintenance of a prisoner sent on board of the guardship. As nothing had been done towards prosecuting him the order came to the comandant to return him to the ship and to present the bill for the expenses incurred in his case. After we had finished our dinner, being very tired from the labor and excitement of the day, we retired to our respective berths, and I soon became oblivious to all things around me until five o'clock next morning.

At five o'clock I arose, called Tom, and after washing ourselves we walked to the market place, where we saw a bewildering display of vegetables and fruit that excelled anything that I had ever seen before. Artichokes, beans, cucumbers, egg plants, lettuce, okra, sweet potatoes, yams and other kinds too numerous to speak of. Of fruit bananas, plantains, limes, oranges, guavas, pomegranates, and many, many others. Poultry in coops; fish dripping from the ocean. To sum it all up it was grand. It was easy to see that dame nature was lavish in her gifts to the people of this favored land. The fountain was throwing out its beautiful stream of water which fell back into the capacious granite basin, cooling the air, and which imparted energy and activity to every living creature within its scope.

We returned to the boarding house, and at eight o'clock we were served with breakfast of mutton chops flavored with limes, fried potatoes, fried plantains, baker's rolls, and coffee. After breakfast Tom admonished the good Frenchman that if any one came to the house to inquire about him to say that he didn't know anything about him. We then went down to the landing and while Tom kept himself *per due* near by, I was on the lookout for the arrival of Capt. Buckland.

About half-past nine o'clock I spied the captain's gig approaching the landing and at once informed Tom of the fact. When the gig arrived at the jetty Capt. Buckland jumped out, followed by his son, and the two waited for Mrs. Buckland to land. Two of the men from the boat followed the captain, presumably to collect the marketing for the day. We now neared the captain, and he soon spied us and motioned us to advance. We hastened to him, hats in hand, and bade him good morning. He said to Tom that as he found that he was so anxious and also, apparently, capable, he had determined to take him. This anxiously desired answer so much pleased Tom that it set him in a tremor of joy and excitement. The captain bade us both to be on board by five o'clock the following morning as he would get under way early in order to take advantage of the land breeze to get out of the harbor.

After we parted from the captain I said to Tom that as he desired seclusion while we remained in Rio, for fear of any more trouble with Capt. Blanchard, that the most feasible way was to go out to the public garden—which was something more than a mile from the city—and pass the day there viewing the grand collection of plants and flowers, fruits and trees of the tropical climes. He gladly agreed to my proposition and we started at once. As we were walking along we came to a baker shop and there bought a loaf of bread, which I tied up in my bandana handkerchief. We walked along and passed by many magnificent villas having extensive grounds lined with shaded walks and flower plats. When we came in view of the public gardens we met a large number of Negresses going into the city, each one carrying a large round basket made of rushgrass, and it filled—some had oranges, while others had bananas. We bought bananas for one hundred reis—about ten cents American money—which afforded us a large supply for the day.

We arrived at the gardens and were admitted by the Brazilian gatekeeper. He asked us what we had in our bundles, and we told him. He said we must leave them at the lodge as it was forbidden to take them into the garden. We at once resigned our bundles to him, and he told us to come for them whenever we desired and we could go out into the roadway and sit under the shade of the road trees and eat our merienda, as he called it. We found the public gardens to be a most instructive and edifying horticultural school. Here we saw growing in all its native luxuriance coffee, tea, nutmeg, allspice, pineapples, mangoes, guavas, and other tropical and semi-tropical fruits. Here we saw the India-rubber tree in all its native luxuriance. As to flowers—they were in variety beyond enumeration—suffice it to say, if you ever heard of a flower it could be found there, with one exception: that was the little flower called the snowdrop. About noon we went to the lodge, took our bread and fruit and passed into the road, sat down under an umbrageous tree and ate our frugal luncheon, with a relish born of healthful appetite. Tom expressed himself as being very happy with the prospect of going so soon to sea again, and still more happy at getting free from the "Samson" and Capt. Blanchard.

As I shall, after this, have no occasion to refer to the ship "Samson," or to Capt. Blanchard again, I will here give a narration of what took place on the ship and what became of the captain.

About six months after my arrival in San Francisco the ship "Samson" arrived, making the passage from Philadelphia in three hundred and eighty-two days. The passengers told me that after the ship sailed from Rio de Janeiro that she became a veritable pandemonium. The captain quarreled with his crew. He quarreled with his passengers, even to fistic encounters; confusion reigned on the ship; the cargo was broached to obtain more liquor, and everything that could add to their misery took place. They were obliged to put into Valparaiso in order to replenish the ship's stores. And after the unprecedented long passage they were glad beyond the power of expression to place their feet on shore in the land of promise.

In about eight months after my arrival, young Brainard arrived in San Francisco and came to see me. He said he staid by his brother until his trial, conviction, and sentence of three years at the quarries—which penal establishment is down the harbor at one of the islands. The good lawyer exerted himself to the utmost, and by his exertions in representing Capt. Blanchard, who was at the trial, in his true colors as a brutal and unscrupulous tyrant, he secured a sentence of comparatively short confinement.

After his brother was taken to the quarries—by the advice of the lawyer and by his aid—he begged an audience with the Emperor. When he was ushered into the royal presence, he threw himself upon his knees, at which the good and kind Emperor said to him: "Rise up, young man, don't kneel to me. Now tell me what your desire is?" Then the youth recounted to the Emperor the history of all his mishaps from the time his father's throat was cut until his brother's trial and conviction. The Emperor said that it seemed that he had been the victim of a concatenation of unfortunate circumstances which had now culminated in branding his brother a felon. All that he could do would be to promise—in case he learned of his brother's good conduct for the next six months—he would grant a pardon so that he again might enter into active life after a salutary lesson by a short imprisonment. He then withdrew from the royal presence, and arranged with the lawyer for his dues to be paid to his authorized agent in San Francisco.

I obtained my goods from the ship, and paid the freight to the agents, Guildermeister, De Fremery & Co., and turned the captain's note in part payment.

The very last I ever heard about Capt. Blanchard was through Tom, the sailor. A ship brought here the bulk of a forty-ton sloop, constructed in Williamsburg, Long Island. She was modeled, set up, and numbered in the frame and planks, and then taken apart, brought around Cape Horn, and put together in San Francisco, at the junction of First and Market streets—which was the margin of the bay at that time. She was named the "San Jose." She was one of three vessels that could reach the Alviso landing; and as Santa Clara valley supplied San Francisco with nearly all the oat hay, these three vessels were coining money. Well, Tom was on the sloop "San Jose," and she was lying at a little wharf called Howison wharf, at the foot of Sacramento street, when one afternoon he was accosted by a tall, corpulent man, whom he recognized as Capt. Blanchard.

Said the captain: "My man, if you will take your yawl boat and scull me off to that ship yonder, I will pay you."

Tom recognized Capt. Blanchard, and answered, " I will take you for nothing, and when I get you well out in the harbor, I'll throw you overboard to Davy Jones, who, I know, will give you a warm welcome."

The captain was astounded with this rude reception, and replied: "What do you mean by such insolence to me, a stranger?" "No," said Tom, "you are not a stranger to me. I am Tom, the sailor who you put on board the guardship in Rio, because I wouldn't let you bullyrag me on board of your ship. Now, we stand here to-day as equals, and you are a great overgrown bully, and if you'll stand up here like a man, I'll knock your blooming mug into the shape of an Admiral's cocked-hat, in the twinkling of a marling spike." Capt. Blanchard, just then, remembered that when a school boy he had read in his lesson that "discretion is the better part of valor," and, for the first time in his life, he thought it was an admirable maxim, and acted upon it forthwith, by walking rapidly to a part of the beach where he was less known and would be better served.

About two weeks after this occurrence I saw in the "Alta California" newspaper that the ship "Samson," Capt. Blanchard, had sailed with passengers for Realejo in the Gulf of Tehuantepec, from whence they were going to cross the land to the Atlantic side and there take ship for their New England homes. I never heard again about Capt. Blanchard or his fortunes.

About eighteen months afterwards a man came to my place of business one day and asked if I still know him. I acknowledged that I did not. He then told me that he was the brother of young Brainard, and also told me that after he had served a period of six months at the penal quarries, the good Emperor had issued a pardon and he had been set free. He then shipped on a vessel that had put into Rio by stress of weather, and she becoming short of hands he had shipped in her and had just arrived in San Francisco. After three months in the northern mines around Nevada, Grass Valley and Rough and Ready, he returned to San Francisco and shipped in a vessel bound for Iquique, Peru, there to load with nitrate for Europe.

This completes the list of all persons on the "Samson," with one exception, and he the best of them all—good old Bryson, who worked on the beach in lighters, taking cargoes from ships in the harbor and putting the goods in store ships which laid near the shore. And I hope and trust that he made his way to his family in Philadelphia with a light heart and a heavy purse.

Now we will return to my story, or as the Frenchmen say, "*revenons a nos moutons.*"

Well, after we had eaten our luncheon of bread and bananas, we returned into the garden and there had a drink of pure water, for which Rio is noted. In the garden was a building, the upper portion of which was a museum containing zoological and ichthyological specimens as well as conchology. We ascended the stairs, which landed us at a balcony. We essayed to go into the museum, but while the attendant allowed me to enter he denied Tom the privilege. I begged to know the reason why he repelled my friend, and he answered that it was because my friend was not wearing a jacket. He then explained to me that while all persons were allowed to enter the garden, the regulations required that every man who entered the museum must wear a jacket. He said that the rule was vigorously enforced, and while he was sorry to deny my friend the privilege of entering the museum, the infraction of the rule would cost him his situation. As my friend, Tom, had an inner shirt and an outer one called a jumper, the wearing of a jacket was considered superfluous. As it was Tom was not permitted to go in, so I declined to enter; we descended the stairs, and as it was four o'clock we started back towards the city.

As strange as the rule seemed to be, I afterwards experienced something just as inexplicable and fully as ridiculous while I was in Liverpool, England. One afternoon a party of us, including three ladies, were walking around in Liverpool, and we went to visit a place called Brown's Library and Museum, which had been established by a wealthy merchant. We had been advised to do so by the landlord of the Victoria Hotel, as it was a place worthy of a visit, and as the admission was free. We presented ourselves at the entrance and as we were about to pass in the doorkeeper espied the parasols in the ladies' hands and at once demanded that they should leave them in his custody while they remained in the building. Two of the ladies immediately yielded up their sunshades, but the third lady, who was more self-asserting than her American sisters, peremptorily refused. The doorkeeper said that was one of the regulations of that institution and he must enforce it. The lady retorted that she had no intention of punching a hole through the pictures, nor of secreting any of the curiosities in her parasol, but while she would have to deny herself the pleasure of entering Brown's Library and Museum, she would have the satisfaction of keeping her parasol in her own hands. So that on account of the lady's obstinacy we were obliged to forego the pleasure of entering Brown's Library and Museum. This episode proved the truth of the old adage, which says:

"When a woman will, she will, you may depend on't;
But when she won't, she won't, and that's an end on't."

This shows that different countries have their own peculiar customs. If you go to Germany, you are obliged to report to the police authorities and tell them from whence you come, what is your business, what is your age and how long you propose to stay, and more than that, what your religion is. In all my travels I have not found any country that affords the freedom of action that equals that which is allowed in the United States. Here a man is allowed to pursue his bent freely, without trammel or restraint.

As we approached the city after our day of seclusion in the garden, Tom became apprehensive of some trap being laid to detain him, but we arrived at our boarding-house unmolested and the landlord told Tom that there had not been any one to inquire about him. We took our dinner of gumbo soup, roast mutton and green peas, with watered claret and coffee. After our long day we were tired enough to turn into our berths, as we would have to rise at half-past four o'clock the next morning. Before we retired I asked the landlord how I could engage a Negro to help to take my chest to the landing so early the next morning, and he kindly told me that he would have two Negroes at hand to do it at a small cost.

I slept very lightly during the night from very gladness for having escaped from the long detention to which I knew the "Samson" would be subjected, and besides the unpleasant associations that were connected with the ship and her captain. The next morning I arose at half-past four o'clock. I called Tom and we prepared ourselves to go aboard of the "Urania." The landlord kindly furnished us coffee and bread, and the two Negroes were at hand to help carry our baggage to the beach. We took leave of the good landlord and started for the beach with our baggage. We engaged a boat and arrived alongside the "Urania" at half-past five o'clock. I went up on deck and made myself known to the mate, who told me to get my dunnage on deck and then myself and Tom should turn to work and lend a hand to get the ship under way. I took my jacket off at once, and after getting our baggage on deck and having settled with the boatman, we at once placed ourselves at the mate's service.

The first order that I received was to lay aloft and loose the maintopsail and overhaul the gear. I sprung up the main rigging with a vim that was born of delight at my deliverance. The anchor had already been hove short and in a few minutes, everything being ready, the order was given to trip the anchor, the jib was hoisted and the ship began to swing. After the three topsails were set, the land breeze having sprung up, we had a fair wind right out of the harbor. Every available sail was now set and the ship passed down the harbor, leaving Forts Santa Cruz and San Juan behind us. Here I was once more on my way to California after having been detained in Rio de Janeiro from December 20th, 1849, to January 22d, 1850.

After the ship was under way the order was passed along for the crew to take their breakfast. I had been so busy that I hadn't time to look about me. But when breakfast was ordered to be eaten some members of the crew came to Tom and myself and welcomed us on board the "Urania," and told us that they hoped that we would find that we had made a good change. We then went down into the forecastle, and as I had neither tin pot for coffee nor pan to eat out of, one of the crew kindly furnished me with them. Our first breakfast on board the "Urania" consisted of fried fresh beef, boiled potatoes, pilot bread and coffee. After breakfast Tom and myself took our baggage and put it down into the forecastle, and as I had no mattress, and the berths being already occupied, two of the crew, who were in the different watches, very kindly agreed to occupy the same berth alternately, and the berth that was thereby vacated was assigned to Tom and myself. The chief mate sent for Tom and me and we went aft in obedience to his order. He told us that the ship was full of passengers, many of whom had never seen salt water before they came on board the ship in Boston, and therefore were ignorant of the usages prevailing on board of a ship at sea. He admonished us against indulging in any familiarity or in any manner offering any affront to any of them. He then told Tom that he would take him into his watch, and he would assign me to the second mate's watch.

After our anchors were stowed and lashed and the chain lowered into the chain-locker, we were ordered to put on the chafing gear and to make everything snug. Whereas the ship that I had just left had thirty-one passengers, this one that I had just come aboard of seemed to have more than one hundred, and the deck appeared to be swarming with men. We were kept busy until twelve o'clock, at which time we were knocked off from work for dinner. Our first dinner on board the "Urania" consisted of soup in which had been boiled a good portion of beef, with an abundance of vegetables; then we had boiled potatoes, plain and sweet, and hard bread. As I was very hungry and very light hearted I ate my fill with a thankful heart, because I was again on my journey to my destination.

I will now describe the ship. The "Urania" was a six-hundred tons ship of modern model, sharp forward with flaring bow, flat on her floor, and a fine, clean run. She was a dry ship at sea, for when a sea struck her forward the spread of her bow was such that the spray was thrown outward. When she was close hauled on the wind she would go through the water, but she was so flat that she didn't hold on, but made a great deal of leeway; but when running free she went like a scared dog. She could knock the socks off of anything that she came alongside of. As a seaboat she was nothing to brag about. She was so flat on the floor that when the wind was abeam and a heavy sea running she would roll to leeward and then come back all standing with a slat and shock that would throw a man aloft right out of the rigging. When she was hove to in a gale she would drift to the leeward so fast that a pint of water couldn't get aboard of her. She was nearly new and as tight as a cup. So it will be seen that I was on board of a fine ship.

The captain hailed from the right arm of the Old Bay State—a man of imposing mien, and, as I learned during the voyage, a gentleman of very few words.

The chief mate, named Ingraham, from Rhode Island, kept himself on the quarter-deck and attended strictly to the sailing of the ship.

The second mate, named Mulroony, was from Nova Scotia, and an active and very ambitious young man.

On board of a ship, when topsails are to be reefed, the place of honor is the weather yardarm, and this position is always accorded by courtesy to the second mate; but when he is disliked some one of the young sailors will run up the rigging for dear life, like a cat, and take the coveted position at the weather ear-ring to the discomfiture of the second mate; but Mr. Mulroony didn't allow any such outgeneraling, for he was always there himself.

The crew of twelve men, I found, had been mostly in coasting vessels, and therefore were not square-riggers, with two or three exceptions. But they were pleasant and very agreeable companions in the forecastle. The steward and the cooks were of the most ordinary kind.

There was a man on board whom they called the ship's doctor. The way this came about was thus: In fitting out a passenger ship for California a great stress was laid upon the sanitary needs of the passengers while they were on such a long voyage of six months or upwards. For that reason the agent of passenger ships would, as an inducement to intending passengers, insert in their advertisements in the newspapers, "A competent physician is engaged to go on the ship to attend to the sanitary needs of the passengers." This announcement would, of course, have great weight in inducing persons to take passage on that ship, but the physician would often prove upon trial to have been an apothecary's clerk, and his knowledge of medicine would be limited to his ability to compound a prescription. Such an one, I understand, was the "Doctor" on board the "Urania." It seems that he had been a clerk with an apothecary in a neighboring town, and having been inspired with a desire to go to the land of gold, had embraced the chance offered to him to sign as "Doctor" on board the "Urania." Thus, with more than one hundred passengers and more than twenty men of the ship's crew, he found himself with a numerous clientage, and therefore a man of importance.

The passengers were of the true New England type, strong, active and intelligent. They were men that had been engaged in such industries as are known to New Englanders—traders, carpenters, stonecutters from Quincy, lumbermen, and a large number of small farmers, many of whom had passed beyond the meridian of the journey of life on their small, comfortable farms, working industriously, living frugally but comfortably, and now, having been enticed by the seductive stories of the lavish wealth in California awaiting the simple effort of the adventurer to yield itself up into his hands, he had left his family to manage the little farm while he sailed to California, from whence he would return with untold riches, when he would settle down to enjoy complete, unalloyed happiness, a condition that has never yet been attained by man. " Man never IS but always TO BE blessed."

The passengers were called the first cabin and second cabin passengers. The first cabin passengers were those in the cabin proper. The second cabin passengers—who composed a community of ninety or more persons—were located in the 'tween decks of the ship, which had been fitted up with berths and tables for that purpose. The forward house was divided into galley, forward part, and passengers' quarters in its after part. On the top of the forward house was an immense longboat, which was turned over and covered with a canvas jacket. Taking it altogether the ship—although somewhat crowded—was far superior to the one which I had left.

At one o'clock all hands were turned out to work and make everything snug for sea. The chains were unshackled from the anchors and lowered into the chain lockers. The water casks were lashed, the fresh provisions stowed away, and the decks cleared up.

Towards evening the breeze began to freshen and the ship moved ahead with good speed. She was so sharp forward that she didn't make the swash that attended the movement of the last ship.

At five o'clock all hands were knocked off for supper, and from that time until eight bells, or eight o'clock, we had nothing more to do than attend to the sheets and braces.

At eight bells the watches were set, and the second mate, into whose watch I had been assigned, had the first watch. The men of our watch drew straws as to who should take the first trick at the wheel, and it fell to me, as I had drawn the shortest straw. I went aft and relieved the man at the wheel, and steered the ship for two hours, when I was relieved by one of my watch-mates.

While I was at the wheel the second mate, Mr. Mulroony, asked me how I came to be adrift in Rio? I replied that I had not been adrift. I then told him that I had engaged my passage on the ship "Samson" to go to San Francisco, and how, by a concatenation of unfortunate circumstances, the ship was detained, and would probably continue in Rio at least three months longer. As soon as he found that I was not a renegade adventurer, he treated me very kindly, and during the voyage had many conversations with me, which I will relate further on.

As I went forward my watch-mate told me about the captain and the mates; saying that the captain had been a successful whaleman who had retired on his well-earned competency, but had been lured by the marvelous stories of the newspapers about the gold fields of California, to go out there, like thousands of others, and add a few more thousands of dollars to his already ample store.

The first mate, they told me, was a silent and strictly attentive man to his duties.

The second mate, in whose watch we were, was a bustling, mercurial character, that was always on the jump, and always on the go.

I found that there were several other ladies on board besides the wife of the captain, who had left home and friends to accompany their husbands on the perilous journey to the newly acquired territory, there to found a new State, and thus to place another star in the azure field of our country's flag.

"A union of seas and union of lands,
  A union of States none can sever;
 A union of hearts and union of hands,
  And the flag of our Union for ever, ever, ever;
   And the flag of our Union for ever."

At eight bells the larboard watch was called, and we were relieved for the next four hours. When we went below I turned into the berth that had been assigned to Tom and myself, and slept a profound, restful sleep.

At eight bells, or four o'clock, our watch was again called on deck, at which time the cooks also went on duty for the day.

At five o'clock we were given a tin pannicken of coffee each, with which we ate a cake of hard bread; after which we turned to work to wash the deck; and thus was the routine work from day to day, when the weather would permit, during the voyage.

When we had been four days at sea we caught a large shark, a regular man-eater, that had been following the ship and showing its fins above water. This is always construed by sailors as an omen of death, as they are said to follow a ship on which some fatality is to occur. The weather now became squally, and thunder and lightning, with a copious fall of rain, kept us busy shortening sail.

It was now January 28th, our position was lat. 27 11 S., long. 44 05 W. The weather had now cleared up, and the wind was nor'west, off the land.

I discovered that the passengers were imbued with true religious fervor, which, no doubt, they had inherited from their puritan ancestors, being transmitted from the days of the landing on Plymouth Rock to the present time.

> "Aye! call it holy ground,
> The spot which first they trod;
> They left unstained what there they found,
> Freedom to worship God."

They held religious meetings, in which each one related his spiritual aspirations, and delivered exhortations on the necessity of self-watchfulness to preserve each one from the commission of sin.

January 29th the wind had so much increased that the order was given to "shorten sail." This went on until the topsails were double reefed, and she was put under reefed foresail, reefed mainsail and jib, foretopmast staysail and reefed spanker. When we were reefing the square sails Mr. Mulroony didn't allow his prestige to wane; for he was at the weather ear-ring every time.

We now heard that a young passenger in the second cabin was very sick from tropical fever. I learned that he had a brother on board who, with others of their fellow-passengers, were assiduously ministering to his wants. They came from the State of Maine, and had left their parents with light hearts and brilliant expectations. Now one of them was stricken down by a most malignant disease. Perhaps, at that very hour, when the absent son is suffering from the burning fever, the fond mother, sitting by her lonely fireside, may be repeating the mournful lines:

"My darling boys now severed far from me,
By many a weary league of land and sea."

But such are the vicissitudes of life; the boy must leave the parental home to fight the battle of life, and to conquer or to fall, when it is so ordered by the divine Ruler.

February 2d we were informed that the young invalid was rapidly sinking under the pressure of the terrible sickness. While he would turn his eyes upon his brother and sympathizing comrades, a sigh would escape from his saddened breast:

"Who to dumb forgetfulness a prey,
    This pleasing, anxious being, e'er resigned;
Left the warm precincts of the cheerful day,
    Nor cast one longing, lingering look behind."

On the following day the sad news spread over the ship that the poor young man had died; had yielded up his spirit to Him who gave it. As one of his comrades repeated: "He has gone to that undiscovered country from whose bourne no traveler returns."

The body of the dead man was at once brought on deck, his bedding thrown overboard, and the 'tween decks was fumigated, to prevent any after consequences. The crew were called to the main hatch, and the body was arranged for burial. On the following day the body was sewed in a canvas shroud and placed on boards, resting on the lee rail, with heavy weights attached. The ship was brought to the wind and hove to; the ensign was set at half-mast, and the ship's bell was tolled. All hands, with bared heads, assembled around the place of the dead, and the captain opened the burial service. "Friends, from the beginning even until now the mournful decree has gone forth into all the earth: 'Dust thou art and unto dust shalt thou return.' One generation passeth away and another generation cometh; and there are few who can hide themselves from the solemn thought, I, too, must die, and the places which know me shall know me no more."

After this exordium the choir of the religious meeting sang the following:

> " Why should we mourn departing friends,
>   Or quake at death's alarm,
> 'Tis but the voice that Jesus sends,
>   To call his children home."

When the singing was concluded, one of the passengers, a leader in the religious meetings, offered a solemn prayer to the Throne of Grace, beseeching that in that awful moment the spirit of the departed one might be received into the mansions of the blest. After the service the body was committed to the mighty deep, amid the lamentations of surviving friends. The body sank into the ocean grave, there to rest until the last trump shall sound.

> " No further seek his merits to disclose,
>   Or draw his frailties from their dread abode;
> There they alike in trembling hope repose,
>   The bosom of his Father and his God."

When the last sad rites had been concluded the ship was filled away and was placed upon her course.

February 8th, lat. 33 10 S., long. 50 02 W., we had been on soundings, hugging the coast, and were now in the latitude of the Rio de la Plata, where we were fearful that we might encounter the much dreaded pampero. We were not disappointed. We had the wind about west nor'west, and were steering south sou'west, with a stiff breeze, and all sail set; when all at once, without premonition, a blast struck the ship that sent her nearly on her beamends. It threw everything into confusion for a moment. The order was given to let go the halyards of the light sails; the courses were hauled up; the topsails lowered to the caps, and everything was taken in as quick as hands could move. The ship soon righted, and was put under close reefed topsails, foretopmast staysail, and mizzen storm trysail. The wind was about west, and the ship could lay her course, and she scooted like a race horse towards Cape Horn.

The gloom that was caused by the recent fatality began to wear off, and the cooling weather had allayed the apprehensions which many had been laboring under; and therefore, a more cheerful spirit seemed to animate every one on the ship.

Our daily fare in the forecastle was passably good. As the captain had supplied a large stock of potatoes, we were enabled to have plenty of salt beef hash, as well as a good dish of lobscouse for breakfast.

Lobscouse is a sea dish and is made of one onion cut and put into one gallon of water, a dozen potatoes peeled and cut into quarters, four cakes of navy bread soaked and broken up. Boil for half an hour. Cut up salt beef into small square pieces equal to one-third of the whole mass, and boil all again half an hour. Then add pepper to taste, and add, when about to be taken up, a half cupful of thickening. On a cold morning it is a dish "fit for the gods!" Just try it.

We frequently had served to us cornmeal mush with molasses. This is a homely dish, but it is mighty satisfying in a cold climate.

The captain now thought of steering the ship between Staten Land and the Coast of Patagonia.

February 18th we sighted Staten Land, lat. 54 42 S., long. 63 43 W. The second mate informed us that Capt. Buckland was intending to sail between the island and the mainland of Patagonia—and this passage is called the Straits of La Maire—thereby making a large gain in distance. We approached Staten Land within about twelve miles distance. As we were sailing along with a light breeze, a shore bird came off and alighted on the main royal yardarm, which to us seemed a harbinger of good luck. The island is mountainous, and showed peaks of perpetual snow.

As night approached the wind hauled to the southward and we were obliged to change our course, and passed outside of Staten Land and between that and Falkland Islands, lat. 51 40 S., long. 57 49 W. During the night the wind was light southerly, and in the morning we were about twenty miles easterly from Staten Land. Towards noon the wind hauled out to the northward, which gave us a fair wind for Cape Horn, lat. 55 58 S., long. 57 49 W.

As we were approaching Cape Horn we sighted many vessels going in the same direction to reach that objective point. These ships had sailed from different Eastern ports, and all going to round Cape Horn. Some of the captains believed in making an eastern passage, that is, to go as far as the longitude of the Azores Islands, long. 31 00 W., then take the trade winds and make a slant for the Patagonian coast, while other captains preferred to take the western passage and just clear Cape Saint Roque. Some of them cross the equator in long. 35 00 W., while other ships cross the equator in long. 25 00 W., hundreds of miles apart, and still these captains are endeavoring to reach Cape Horn in the quickest way that each thinks is possible. After they have rounded Cape Horn and have reached their destined port they don't quarrel about the route that each took to accomplish the desired result. Here is a lesson that some of our devout religious teachers might study with benefit to themselves and edification to their flocks. How can they expect those who hear them say from the pulpit, "Be not contentious; on the contrary be humble and submissive, as our divine teacher was submissive." This is good doctrine, but in order to make good teaching effective the teacher himself should first set the example. Why should the teacher, in speaking to his flock, attack in the most acrimonious manner all other teachers who don't teach just as he teaches? He thereby creates a spirit of contention which is not conducive to religious edification. If there are little differences in religious belief, let us not be constantly inveighing against those that differ from us, but practice a spirit of conciliation and amity as the captains do that steer their ships for Cape Horn but pursue a somewhat different course to reach the same end. And at the end of the voyage of life may we hope and trust that it may be said to each and every one of us, " Well done, thou good and faithful servant."

"Judge not the Lord by feeble sense,
But trust him for his grace."

We were now experiencing pretty cold weather and after having been in the tropics so long it affected us quite sensibly. We asked the second mate for permission to make coffee each night at seven bells, that is, at half-past eleven, as then after the watch on deck had taken their coffee there still would be a supply for the other watch which came on deck at eight bells or midnight. He readily granted our request and we went to the galley and made the coffee. On the second night, the larboard watch having the first watch on that night, prepared the coffee, and when the starboard watch came on deck we took our share. Well, on this night a sheet of gingerbread had been left in the galley by the cook, and some one of the sailors had abstracted it and divided it among his mates. On the next night the galley was found to have been locked. We informed the second mate and he lodged a complaint with the captain. The captain sent for the steward and ordered him to have the galley left unlocked every night until the ship got around Cape Horn. The steward, as a matter of course, had the cook to leave the galley unlocked.

Three nights after the second opening of the galley it was our first watch on deck; we started the fire in the caboose and made the coffee. One of our watch found a sheet of gingerbread and appropriated it. We had been ordered not to touch anything in the galley but the coffee. The cake was broken and passed around. I was offered a piece, which I took and examined by the lamp and found that it contained particles that sparkled in the light. I pointed out the peculiar appearance to my watchmates and declined to eat, and some others of the watch also refused to eat the queer looking cake. But three men and the second mate ate heartily of the sweet bread. At twelve o'clock, midnight, the larboard watch was called; we were relieved and went below. About two bells, one o'clock, I was awakened by one of my watchmates groaning and moaning. In five minutes thereafter another was attacked in the same way, and then the third one. The ones who were not affected were the ones who had not eaten of the gingerbread. The chief mate, whose watch it was, came to the forecastle gangway and asked what was the matter. He was told that the men appeared to be very sick. He ordered one of the men to go aft and call the "Doctor." In the meantime the sick men had been attacked with violent purging and vomiting. When the messenger returned forward he brought the news that the second mate had been attacked in a similar manner. The affair had now become so serious that Capt. Buckland was called. The "Doctor" came forward and pronounced it a case of indigestion from having eaten too much, and said that the men would be all right by morning. But by morning the men and the second mate were much worse than they were when first attacked. When the passengers began to come on deck and heard of what had occurred they began to discuss the matter in a very serious manner. As the "Doctor" was the person that had charge of the medicine chest, and the men who had eaten of the cake were the only ones affected, the question very naturally arose whether it was that the cake had been doctored. One of the men of the crew went aft to the quarter deck and boldly asked the "Doctor" if he had put any drug into that cake. Capt. Buckland felt his dignity as captain of the ship insulted, and having before had a conference with the "Doctor," answered for him and said that what had been done was done by his order. This put quite a different face upon the affair. In the meantime it had leaked out that the "Doctor" had acknowledged to the captain that he had, with the connivance of the steward, put some emetic powder in the cake in order to punish the sailors for purloining food from the galley to which they had no right. But Capt. Buckland soon learned that he had made a most serious mistake in assuming the responsibility for the nefarious act of the "Doctor." All that day the men were very sick. The violent purging and vomiting had relieved them from the severe pains, yet they were very sick. The passengers felt that while they had a man in their midst who was capable of perpetrating such an atrocious act, and that man was sustained by the captain, that no man on board, neither passenger nor sailor, was safe from the dangerous schemes of the secret enemy.

At last the passengers met in convention, elected a chairman, secretary and sergeant-at-arms. After reviewing the situation the men of cool judgment and moderate views advised the arrest and confinement of the "Doctor," while the younger and more noisy portion demanded that the culprit be tried at once, and if proven guilty of conspiring to poison the crew, that he be hanged at once or thrown overboard. These hot blooded, fiery young fellows reminded me of Shakespeare's description of young manhood:

" Then a soldier; full of strange oaths, and bearded like the pard;
Jealous in honor, sudden and quick in quarrel;
Seeking the bubble reputation even in the cannon's mouth."

The moderate counsel prevailed and the "Doctor" was immediately arrested by the sergeant-at-arms.

How often have I been reminded in after years, when I saw the first vigilance committee of 1852, and the one of 1856, that men, when the emergency arises, can quickly adopt measures for self-protection.

The captain was called upon to furnish handcuffs and the "Doctor" was manacled and confined to his room under guard. The victims of the diabolical scheme were invalided for about ten days, after which time they returned to duty. As to the "Doctor," he was kept in confinement for several days, after which time, as the captain had taken charge of the ship's medicine chest, and therefore had rendered the

"Doctor" unable to perpetrate any further mischief, he was released from confinement and allowed his freedom. But he never, during the balance of the voyage, ventured to go forward of the mainmast.

During all these exciting events I was surprised to notice that the steward, who to my mind was far from being blameless, was not called to account for the part he had enacted, nor was he deposed from the important position of being steward of the ship. Whatever secret influence he possessed, it was sufficient to save him from being taken to account for his participation in the affair.

The second mate, Mr. Mulroony, was very depressed and melancholy for a time, but after awhile his buoyancy of spirits asserted itself and he became as active as before the unpleasant episode. We, the sailors, continued to make our coffee, for the weather was very severe and cold, but we never after searched the galley for any more tidbits, as the severe lesson was very effective.

February 20th, by noon observation our position was lat. 55 07 south, long. 64 03 west. The weather was very cold and the sky was overcast with heavy dark clouds. At four P. M. the captain ordered that the royal yards be sent down on deck. This was an act of precaution that showed that he was preparing for much worse weather and more of it. The wind was now west-southwest, and we were plunging along under double-reefed topsails and reefed courses, jib and foretopmast staysail. The sea from the westward was very heavy, but the captain kept all the sail on the ship that she could bear, as she was laying her course. By six P. M. the royal yards had been sent down on deck, and then the order came to rig in the flying-jibboom. We rigged this in as far as the head stays allowed and lashed it to the jibboom, and tautened the head stays and guys and lashed the sail snug.

It was now eight bells and we were allowed to eat our supper. After supper the larboard watch turned in, as we had the first watch on deck. The night did not set in before nine P. M. in these high latitudes at this time of the year.

At four bells, ten P. M., it was my trick at the wheel. The ship was plunging and pitching in the heavy sea, but she was as dry as a chip on deck and steered very easy.

At six bells, eleven o'clock, everything around was enveloped in a dark haze, and the wind was whistling through the rigging. Every few moments the ship would give a lurch to leeward which would cause the second mate, who was walking on the weather side of the quarter-deck, to grasp the mizzen rigging, if he missed which he would slide against the trunk of the cabin with a thump. We had our starboard tacks aboard and were heading south by west. All at once the man on the lookout sung out in thundering tones, "Sail ho!" and before another word was said there appeared on our weather beam an immense black body that was rushing and bearing right down upon us at lightning speed and with a thundering whir.

The second mate called out, "Hard up your helm; ring the ship's bell!" One of the watch—who had been reading Capt. Marryatt's novel, "The Phantom Ship"—cried out, in his terror, "'Tis the Flying Dutchman!" One of the watch grabbed the cook's axe, and began to pound the anchor. The mate and captain rushed on deck, but by the time they had reached the deck there was nothing to be seen. For what we saw was like a flash of lightning. It was a ship under topsails and courses, steering east nor'east, right before wind, and just passed so near our weather quarter that they could have tossed a biscuit on board of our ship, but was now lost in the gloom of the night. This gave us a great fright, but it was no fault of ours. We were on the lookout, but our ship had no side-lights, for at that time they were not used, unless sailing up or down a river.

Capt. Buckland instructed the second mate to keep a sharp lookout, as we were directly in the track of vessels going east around Cape Horn from the Western Coast of America and from Australia.

Our time had been so much occupied by the passing ship that we had to do without our midnight coffee.

Some of the passengers were so much disturbed by this

affair that they passed the balance of the night on deck. The weather was now boisterous and disagreeable, with frequent showers of rain.

After leaving Rio the crew were kept on deck all afternoons for three days while everything was made snug for sea. After which time we were allowed "watch and watch," and whatever was to be done about deck or aloft was performed by the watch that was on deck, unless in a case of emergency, when "all hands on deck" was called out; at which times we were required to work until the watch was ordered below. This gave us ample leisure to sleep, to read, and to mend our clothes.

The potatoes were now exhausted, and we were obliged to fall back on bread scouse, and Indian meal mush for breakfast; but we had good beef, and real corn-fed pork, which, with plenty of beans, codfish and rice, we fared very well in the forecastle.

February 22d, "Washington's Birthday," lat. 56 23 S., long. 70 03 W., wind still west to west sou'west, but more moderate. Shook the reefs out of the topsails and courses and set the main staysail and spanker. Steering south by west close hauled. The ship sailed well but making large leeway.

The second mate said the captain would run the ship to 59 south and then 'bout ship and go on the other tack. Today, when the haze cleared off, sighted a ship to the windward steering on the wind, like ourselves, but while we outsailed her she could out-weather us, as she kept her grip better.

Our ship was sometimes surrounded by right whales, as their locality is in high latitudes, where the temperature of the water is cold; as the sperm whale is seen in low latitudes where the temperature of the water is warm.

There were two young sailors in the crew who had been whaling, and when they would see a whale rise up to the surface of the water and spout out a volume of water, they would sing out, "There she blows!" Then they would say: "Ah! boys, I wish we had a cedar lapstreak whaleboat with whaling gear; how I'd like to fasten on to one of them fellers and then just have him tow the boat through the water, like a streak of greased lightning. I tell you its fine fun." But I thought it was far better in its omission than it would be in its observance. This desire, expressed by the quondam whaleman, proved the truth of the old saying, "that when a person has once been in an occupation that was fraught with danger that when the same conditions present themselves afterwards that the impulse to rush into the fray becomes irresistible." However, as we had no lapstreak whaleboat nor whaling gear on board, my shipmate could not indulge the bent of his inclination.

February 25th, lat. 59 06 S., long. 75 11 W. The wind had hauled to the southward, it now being southwest. At four bells, 2 P. M., we went about in stays, and the wind having somewhat moderated, the topgallantsails were set, and the maintopmast staysails. The ship was close hauled, heading about west northwest, and as Cape Horn was in lat. 55 58, the captain hoped to pass it with a wide berth.

To-day there was a school of porpoises around the ship, and after throwing the harpoon several times, by one of the crew, one of these denizens of the briny deep was captured and hauled on deck. After the blubber was stripped off the meat was cut into slices, parboiled, and then wiped dry and fried in pork fat. The meat was quite palatable in this way but not equal to what it is when made into minced balls.

February 26th. To-day we had a change of wind. It backed around from southwest to south and then to southeast, giving us a free wind, steering west. We now began to make longitude, having Cape Horn well under our lee. On the twenty-sixth day of February we caught an albatross with a baited hook, which was towing on the surface of the sea. When it was hauled on board and the hook taken from its bill, it was allowed to walk around on deck, as it could not rise from the deck. The albatross is an immense bird with a large body, and a spread of wings from eight to fourteen feet. This was a very large bird. One of the passengers took a strip of sheet copper and engraved upon it the name of the ship, date and latitude. He then bored a hole through one end of the sheet and passed a strong leather thong through the same. He then passed it around the upper joint of the wing of the bird and sewed the ends together. Then the bird could fly, and he could eat without any detriment to his movement. After this was done he was taken up from the deck and allowed to fly away.

Now the sequel of this affair was most singular. When we arrived in San Francisco and had been in port about ten days, what was our surprise to see in the "Boston Journal," steamer edition, a paragraph relating the circumstance of the capture of the albatross, by a ship that afterwards touched at Valparaiso, and had sent the news to Panama by the English mail steamer, whence it was taken to New York by the Pacific mail steamer, conveying the news to anxious friends that the voyagers were safe on the ocean. This remarkable incident clearly comes within the category of cases in which it is said that, "truth is stranger than fiction."

We were now in the Pacific Ocean—the great Pacific—the peaceful, quiet, calm ocean. Although it was not so quiet, just then, on that 29th day of February, 1850, lat. 56 02 S., and long. 77 10 W., still we felt certain as we progressed northerly and left the "Southern Cross" behind us, that the weather would be improved by the lowering of our latitude. Every one on board the ship now began to show a brighter face, with one exception—that was the "Doctor." I cannot say that he showed a brighter face, because he did not show his face, as he was still in "durance vile." Our course was now northerly; and it was learned in the forecastle that the captain had made up his mind to touch at the Island of Juan Fernandez, made historic and impressed deeply in the mind of almost every boy in America and in England by the simple and romantic story of Alexander Selkirk, or better known as "Robinson Crusoe." That was the first book of travel which I ever read, and, when reading it, how I longed and wished that I could have been on that romantic island, dressed in goat skins, cultivating the little garden, training the kids and watching the ocean's birds that landed there to hatch their young. And now, so many years afterwards, I was to see that island.

I remember that after I had read the little book I loaned it to an old lady of the neighborhood where I lived, and when she returned it to me, after having read it, she shed tears of sympathy for poor Crusoe, because of his sufferings on that lonely island in mid-ocean.

We were now ordered to send up the royal yards and to run out the flying jib-boom. The wind had again hauled back to the south'ard and eastward, and as our course was now northward and westward we had a free wind. We now began to enjoy the benefits of pleasant weather. The passengers now began to come on deck and gather in groups for conversation.

At this time the feeling between the people of the free and slave States was becoming very rancorous, arising entirely from the question of freedom versus slavery. The people of the northern States deprecated the condition of our country, arising from the existence of slavery in our nation; while the people of the southern States insisted upon its maintenance, and compelled the national government to enact laws for its protection and perpetuation in the new territories acquired by purchase or conquest.

Even in the Territory of California up to the day of its admission as a State of the Union, the southern masters had brought many of their slaves for the purpose of having them labor in the mines, thereby to enrich their masters. But the masters very soon learned that they had made a very serious mistake, for the sons of the heroes of Bunker Hill gave them to understand that vassal or slave would not be allowed to be held in bondage by a master, and breathe the same air that a free-born American did. When the owners of human slaves were convinced of this fact, they, by force of circumstances, were obliged to give up the contest and retire to the State from whence they came.

I had seen in Charleston, South Carolina, negro cooks and stewards, that came there on board of ships that had come to load with cotton for Europe, taken out of the ship by the sheriff of the county and placed in jail and there detained until the ship was ready to go to sea. Then they would be returned to the ship, and a bill would be presented to the captain for their maintenance during their enforced seclusion. This, they claimed, was done to prevent the free Negroes of the North from infusing into the minds of the slaves the mischievous sentiment of human freedom that was so prevalent in the Northern States.

The National Government was so much dominated over by the southern slave holders that when complaints were sent to Washington by the merchants of the North, they were thrown into the waste basket to be swept out the following morning by the Negro slave of the Secretary of the Treasury.

The passengers on board the "Urania" were men who had obtained their education in that great diffuser of knowledge, the "District School," which they had attended for three months in each year, commencing the first Monday after Thanksgiving Day, and continuing in session for three months in each year. The balance of nine months they were obliged to work in order that the family pot might be kept boiling. In the school they were taught reading, writing, arithmetic, geography and grammar. After the age of twenty-one years a male scholar was not allowed in the district school.

If a rich man desired a higher education for his son, there were the academies and the colleges open to them, but the taxpayer was not required to pay for the rich man's son to obtain that higher education, which he could not afford to give to his own son.

All the passengers were constant readers, and I was informed that they were well supplied with instructive books. There were two men among the number that particularly attracted my attention. One was named Hiram Bardell and the other Zeno Scudder. They possessed a quadrant and a Bowditch's Navigator between them, and they could be seen every clear day on the topgallant forecastle taking a noon-day observation of the sun. After the altitude of the sun was obtained at meridian, they would get the Bowditch's Navigator and work out the latitude. Then they reckoned out the longitude by dead reckoning. They ascertained the course steered the previous twenty-four hours and the distance sailed; then they made due allowance for leeway and course of the current. By one o'clock each afternoon they would have their bulletin ready for the information of their fellow-passengers as to the position of the ship and her distance from San Francisco.

March 2d. The wind has changed to the northeast, with a moderate breeze. Our position by observation at noon was lat. 53 05 S., long. 76 15 W. We are now standing with our larboard tacks aboard and heading along about E. by S. to E. S. E. To-day our amateur navigators were asked as to the position of the ship, and Mr. Bardell promptly answered, "lat. 57 18 south, long. 77 45 west." Well, this was thought pretty close for midocean, but it would not do to sail a ship by in approaching the land. However, it occupied their time and served to beguile the time that would otherwise hang heavy on their hands.

The passengers, some of whom have boats on board the ship, are now talking about what they will do when they arrive in San Francisco. It seems to be their intention to start directly for the mining region and commence the accumulation of their fortune at once.

There was one man in the forecastle whose name was Cyrenus Eldridge, but he was called Uncle Cy. He was a man considerably advanced in years and very good natured and quiet. He, it seems, was an old and valued acquaintance of the captain, and for that reason had been shipped on board the "Urania" as an able seaman, but he was not required to go aloft. He became quite communicative to me and revealed to me his condition. He said that his home was on the shores of Buzzard's Bay, Cape Cod; that he owned a modest little farm of a few acres, which was situated on the borders of the bay where there was an indentation which made a nice safe harbor for his boat. He raised all the potatoes, corn, turnips, pumpkins and other vegetables that he needed; besides he had a few apple and quince trees, which supplied a reasonable quantity of fruit. In the summer time he could take his little boat and go out on the bay and catch the tautog, scuppaug and bluefish; in the winter he could take his spear and spear all the eels that his family could use. But there was an incubus hanging upon him and his little family in the shape of a six hundred dollars mortgage. He told me that if he could in the space of one or two years accomplish the feat of discharging that mortgage, it would place him in a condition that would be superior to that of the great Daniel Webster on his Marshfield farm. And now I pen this with the liveliest satisfaction, that within one year after we arrived in California Uncle Cy called upon me in San Francisco and informed me that he had accomplished the purpose of his tedious voyage around Cape Horn—had already sent the money by Adams & Co.'s Express to discharge the mortgage, and also had enough with him to pay his way home and have something left after he arrived there. He left San Francisco in a ship bound to Realejo, in the Gulf of Tehauntepec, to cross from thence to the Atlantic side, and from there to Boston. Good Cyrenus Eldridge, it is my sincere hope that he has realized his most sanguine expectations.

The wind continued northeast for two days, and as we could not lay closer than east by south, we found ourselves in lat. 54 51 S., long. 65 30 W. The weather was still sharp and chilly, but the midnight coffee had now been stopped, and the "Doctor" would never get another chance at the crew.

March 8th the wind hauled around to southeast, giving us a fair wind, and we shaped our course north-northwest for Juan Fernandez. "Hurrah!" said the passengers. "Hurrah!" said the crew. As the atmosphere was clear and the barometer indicated good weather, the captain ordered that every stitch of canvas be put on the ship. We ran out the topmast and to'gallant stun'sail booms and set the sails; the mainsail was hauled up and the two lower stun'sails set. As the "Urania" had no swinging booms, the lower stun'sails were not as effective as they would have been in the old style, for a lower stun'sail when not kept in place by a boom may roll up into a scroll like a sheet of paper. When every rag that could draw was put on to her I think the "Urania" reeled off about fourteen knots. She was a wonderfully fast sailor with the wind aft.

We now began to lower our latitude rapidly, and the passengers began to furbish up their guns so as to be ready to bring down a score or two of the famous goats that were left on Juan Fernandez by Robinson Crusoe.

March 12th, lat. 40 10 S., long. 71 05 W. The wind is steady, southeast, and the second mate says that we will reach Juan Fernandez in three days' time if the wind holds as now. The passengers are anticipating a pleasure season on shore when we reach Juan Fernandez.

March 15th. We are now nearing the romantic island; our position at 12 meridian was 34 42 S., long. 76 03 W. The captain ordered the second mate to send a man aloft to keep a lookout for land, as Juan Fernandez has very high, mountainous peaks. At eight bells in the evening the captain ordered all the light sails to be taken in, the mainsail to be hauled up and furled, and put the ship under topsails, foresail and jib.

The next morning we put all sail on the ship and away she went, steering northwest with the wind dead aft. As soon as it was daylight a man was ordered aloft to look out for land or sail.

At seven bells our watch was called and the cook gave us for breakfast bread scouse, fried pancakes and coffee. At eight o'clock our watch went on duty, and I was ordered to go aloft and relieve the man on the lookout. After I had relieved the man of the larboard watch I settled myself on the foretopmast crosstrees and scanned the horizon carefully, in the hope that I might have the honor of sighting the land; but for the two hours that I was on the lookout neither land nor sail did I see.

At four bells I was relieved and descended to the deck. The passengers gathered around me and asked whether I had seen the land, and when I answered in the negative they turned from me disappointed. Every passenger seemed to be on deck, and it was with some difficulty that the crew could pass around in obedience to orders given from the quarter-deck.

About six bells the lookout aloft proclaimed the joyful news, "Land ho! land ho!" "Where away?" asked the captain. "Three points on the larboard bow, sir." "Very well: come down." "Aye, aye, sir," and the lookout man came on deck.

"Put your helm to starboard and bring her up two points," said the captain. "Aye, aye, sir," responded the man at the wheel. The excitement among the passengers was wonderful to behold. They seemed to feel that they were approaching towards the end of their journey, although they were still thousands of miles away from it, but the idea of having reached Juan Fernandez made the balance of the journey seem easy.

At 2 P. M., having reached what appeared to us to be quite near the island, Capt. Buckland ordered the first mate to launch the yawl boat and have her manned, and to go and reconnoiter the island for the purpose of finding a suitable place for an anchorage. We got the yawl boat into the water, after bringing the ship up into the wind, and four of the crew were ordered into the boat, Tom and myself being among them. The chief mate took charge of the boat, taking two of the after-cabin passengers with him for company. We pulled away from the ship and steered for the shore, under the supposition that it was about five miles distant. After we had rowed about a mile from the ship we discovered that the boat was leaking very copiously, and we, the sailors, had all we could do to pull the boat, and as the mate had to steer her, the two passengers had no alternative but to bail out the water or let the boat sink. When they found that it was either bail or sink, they took hold and worked for dear life. Well, we rowed, and we rowed, and we rowed, and the longer we rowed the further the land seemed to be from us. Well, after a long and tedious trip we neared the land, but we found that the sea was breaking furiously all along the shore, and that the coast was bold and perpendicular; we rowed along from the eastern point and went westerly until we arrived at a very bluff promontory, which we passed, and came in view of an indentation that formed quite a bay, with a shelving, sandy beach. The mate exclaimed, "Eureka! We have found it." We learned afterwards that this roadstead was known as Cumberland Bay.

After a long pull, which had nearly exhausted us, and about used up the two passengers, we made a landing, finding ourselves safe on shore, drenched through and through with the spray, and entirely without water or food. And it was now past 7 o'clock by the mate's watch.

After we had beached our boat and drawn her well up on the sand, we began to look around us. We first looked towards our ship which we saw was well in the offing, and we had learned, to our cost, that instead of being five miles from shore when we started that we had been at least fifteen miles distant from it. We looked up inland, and there, to our delight, we saw what appeared to be three diminutive houses, from one of which we could see smoke issuing.

As we walked up towards the little settlement we could see one or two men, who had probably spied us, coming towards us. As they were approaching us I could see that one of them was a pale, sharp-faced man, with carroty hair, while the other was a swarthy, corpulent man, with black hair and large, dark eyes, that looked kindly upon us. The carroty haired man gave the usual Yankee salutation, "How de doo," to which the mate made the characteristic reply, "Pretty well, I thank you." The swarthy man inclined his head condescendingly, and they both advanced and met us. The mate shook hands with them both, and entered into conversation with carrot-head. He told him that the ship in the offing was the ship "Urania," from Boston, with passengers to the number of more than one hundred; that the two gentleman, then present, were of the number, while the others, pointing to us, were members of the crew. The

Islander introduced himself as being a New England whaleman, who had been landed there from the ship "Gideon Howland," of New Bedford, he being at the time suffering from the scurvy, caused by the excessive use of salt food. He introduced his companion as being Don Eusebio Domingo de Echandea, Gobernador de Juan Fernandez. When we learned the title of the gentleman, who was standing before us, we at once raised our hats, to which salutation he courteously responded. The mate then made known the object of this visit to be to obtain a supply of water and wood sufficient to enable us to complete our voyage to San Francisco. To his inquiries satisfactory answers were given; but, as it was out of the question to return to the ship that night, the Yankee whaleman offered us a shelter for the night in one of the small houses. The mate gladly accepted the kind offer, as the ship was out of sight, owing to the darkness. We secured the boat for the night, and then we followed our entertainer to the little hut, where we were permitted to build a fire on the earth floor. As I said before, we had not taken either water or food with us—which was very imprudent, and very short-sighted on the part of the captain, as he had been a whaleman and knew the necessity of providing for such contingencies as getting benighted at sea in a boat. But the whaleman told us that a number of vessels that were bound to California had touched there to obtain wood and water, and in return for such service as he had rendered they had rewarded him with a generous supply of hard bread and other articles, from the land of civilization. He kindly gave us some of his store of hard bread and also some dried fish. We ate of his bounty, and started a fire, and made ourselves a bed, of rushes and grass, for the night; while the mate and his two friends were supplied with goat skins. During the night the wind increased to a gale, and blew around the house of sticks and rushes with a mournful sound.

As we were worn out with our severe labor of the day, we could exclaim, with Sancho Panza, "Blessings on the man who invented sleep." As we all fell asleep, and the fire had burned out, when we awoke towards morning we were chilled to the very marrow—as some of us had not even taken a jacket along. When we aroused up and went outside the hut we found that the wind was blowing at a speed of forty miles an hour, and it was attended with a drizzling rain. As the weather was thick we couldn't see the ship in the offing, and therefore we had to bide our time to get aboard again. In this dilemma the mate obtained a couple of fishing lines, and as the whaleman told him that small fish were plentiful a short distance from the shore, he had us launch the boat, and he and his two passenger friends got into the boat, with two of my shipmates to row the boat, and he told myself and my other shipmate to gather some branches of wood and obtain some kind of a kettle from our benefactors wherein to cook the fish, if they caught any. We gathered the wood and started the fire. I then approached Don Eusebio, the Governor, and asked him, in his own language, the favor of a loan of a vessel that would be suitable to cook the fish. As this was the first time that I had spoken, he was surprised to hear me address him in his own language. He took me up to his house and gave me an iron pot, also some salt, and became quite communicative. He told me that he was the son of a Spaniard that had come to Chili from Santander, Spain, and had married and settled in Valparaiso, where he, the son, was born. While he was yet a small boy his father removed his family to Santiago, where he was appointed to a government position. His father had died while he was yet a boy, and for that reason he had not obtained that preferment which his father, if living, could easily have obtained for him. After he was married he had enjoyed a clerkship in a government office until his predecessor, as Governor of Juan Fernandez, had asked to be relieved, on account of his growing children, whom he desired to have educated, and for that reason he wished to resign, and return to the mainland.

At this juncture, as the government did not desire to leave the island entirely unprotected, for fear that some other nation might be tempted to take possession for strategic purposes, the position had been offered to him at a salary that was small but still adequate to supply all his moderate wants. He said that the government sent a vessel once every year with supplies, and his family and one man, which the government allowed, comprised the force that held the island. He then showed me his commission, which was headed, "Don Eusebio Domingo de Echandea, Gobernador de Juan Fernandez, bajo el gobierno de Chile." I told him that I had been in Santander, where his father was born; that I went there from New Orleans, in a vessel loaded with leaf tobacco. I told him that Santander was near Santoña, a naval station on the coast of the Bay of Biscay, and an extensive naval arsenal. When I proved to him that I knew of what I was speaking, he declared that had he known it when I landed he would have furnished me with the softest goat skins and a warm corner in his own house. He then called to his daughter Casilda and introduced me as a person who had been in the very place where her grandfather was born. Casilda was about fifteen years of age, and appeared to be very unsophisticated and childish. She neither saluted me nor even spoke to me. Soon the carroty-headed whaleman came to where we stood and gave me such a withering look that I was glad to return to my work and set the pot to boiling. About nine o'clock the boat, which had been within hailing distance all the time, came ashore, and we found that the fishing party had met with good success.

As the water was already boiling and seasoned with salt, we soon cleaned the fish and boiled them. On the mate's promise to return him tenfold the whaleman gave us a few more cakes of hard bread, and we had a grand breakfast of boiled fish and bread.

About eleven o'clock the wind moderated and the haze lighted. We soon obtained a sight of the ship a long distance to the northward of the island. As the wind was fair for us to reach her, the mate ordered the boat to be launched and away we went, the mate promising the whaleman and the Governor that we would soon return with the ship. We now had the advantage of a fair wind and the sea right after us, with plenty of daylight ahead.

We arrived on board the ship about two o'clock, and as soon as the boat was hoisted out of the water the boat's crew was allowed to go below and have their dinner. After we had gone down into the forecastle our shipmates told us that when the passengers found that we didn't return by dark, they advised and desired the captain to put the ship before the wind, and let the boat's crew follow on the next ship that might touch at the island. This the captain flatly refused to do, but put the ship under close-reefed topsails and stood off and on until the weather cleared up the next day.

It took us until noon the next day to reach the anchorage. As soon as we anchored in fifteen fathoms of water, rocky bottom, all hands were put to work to prepare rafts of casks to take ashore and fill with fresh water, which we found to be good and abundant, running in cascades from the mountains. The way we prepared our raft of casks was thus: A cask was taken and a quarter hoop was started at each end; under each of these hoops was placed a small becket on each side and then the hoop was driven back to its place. Through these beckets was passed a strong rope on six or eight casks—a rope on each side of the casks. This makes a strong raft. Then the boat takes it in tow and it is taken ashore to the beach, where each cask is filled and bunged tight. When all the casks in the raft are filled the raft is towed back to the ship and each cask is hooked on to in its turn with canhooks or else put in slings and hoisted on deck. The crew were kept busy in getting the water and the wood on board.

The island we found to be a veritable paradise. It is of a lava formation and shows that it was in some remote age thrown up by some terrible convulsion of nature out of the bowels of the earth, until it reached an altitude of at least five thousand feet in places, and the peaks looked as symmetrical and shapely as church spires. It was divided into alcoves, with high, precipitous promontories for sides, and it required the use of a boat to go from one recess to the next one.

The place of anchorage was in front of a charming sylvan

spot of about a mile and a half frontage, facing the ocean and reaching back by a gentle rise about three-quarters of a mile to the foot of inaccessible cliffs. This little valley was a real paradise. It was bounded by umbrageous trees as well as stocked with fruit trees of many varieties. Peaches were at this time in their full maturity; quinces so large that they astonished the farmers who had emigrated from the bleak northern hemisphere; wild oats in the fullness of harvest time; figs to be had for the picking. In a word it was a most beautiful oasis in midocean.

Of animals there were wild horses, cattle, hogs, goats and dogs. One of these dogs was brought here on board of another ship by a gentleman named Tarbett, and he named him Juan. He was captured when young. He was fawn-colored, and was gentle and very affectionate to his master. Although all these animals were there, not a cow nor a horse had Governor Echandea in domesticity; they were all wild and unconfined.

JUAN FERNANDEZ.

Juan Fernandez is in lat. 33 37 south and long. 78 43 west. It is distant about three hundred and seventy miles from Chile, to which republic it belongs. The climate is similar to that of South Carolina, excepting the intense South Carolina heat of midsummer. It was at one time a penal colony, where prisoners were kept in banishment for a period. The caves wherein they lived were still to be seen, and it was from this circumstance that so many horses and cattle were there, as when the garrison and the prisoners were withdrawn the few horses and cattle were left behind and since that time had increased wonderfully in that genial climate.

Our passengers formed themselves into gunning parties and sallied forth with anticipations of successful sport, but they returned disappointed, for when they sighted the game it was on some inaccessible cliff, so that, although it was killed, it would fall into an abyss from whence it could not be recovered. Although the hunters returned to the ship with empty game bags, such was not the case with the passengers who went out in the boat to the fishing ground, a cable length from the ship. Their catching of the fish was limited only by the capacity of the cooks to fry them. We had fried fish at every meal while we were in the harbor. After such a dearth of fresh food the supply of abundance of fish and fruit was truly a delicious feast.

After two days of incessant labor, at noon on the third day the wood and the water were got on board, and then the captain told the mate to give the crew a half holiday until six P. M., at which time he would weigh anchor.

As Governor Echandea had told us that the cave of Robinson Crusoe was about one and a half miles to the westward, in a small cove that could be easily reached by a boat, but would take a day to go by land, we asked the mate for permission to use one of the boats for the purpose. We accordingly took the boat, and four of us rowed around the promontory into the cove of which I had read so much in the delightful story of Robinson Crusoe. The little cove is a repetition of the one where the ship was laying, but very diminutive in size. The cave was a few rods from the margin of the sea, on an elevation opening towards the sea, and from which the recluse had a full view, and a visual sweep of the ocean.

It was here that the poor shipwrecked mariner passed four lonely years of his adventurous life. It was here that he trained his goats, watched the seafowls and the wild beasts that roamed around on the precipitous cliffs. It was on this very spot that he had cultivated his little garden. The poor fellow! I could almost picture him as standing before me, with his unique garments of goat skins, looking, with longing eyes, out upon the broad expanse of ocean to, perchance, discover some friendly sail, that might be directed hitherward by a kind Providence, to rescue the poor shipwrecked mariner.

While contemplating this beautiful glade, interspersed with peach and quince trees, the pathetic lines of Crusoe's poem occurred to my mind:

> " I'm monarch of all I survey,
>   My right there is none to dispute,
> From the center, all round to the sea,
>   I'm lord of the fowl and the brute.
>
> O! solitude where are the charms,
>   That sages have seen in thy face.
> Better dwell in the midst of alarms,
>   Than reign in this horrible place.
>
> I'm out of humanity's reach,
>   I must finish my journey alone.
> Never hear the sweet music of speech,
>   I start at the sound of my own.
>
> The wild fowl has flown to her nest,
>   The wild beast has gone to his lair.
> Even here there's a season of rest,
>   And I must to my cabin repair.
>
> There's mercy in every place,
>   And mercy encouraging thought
> Gives even affliction a grace,
>   And reconciles man to his lot."

As we had no timepiece with us the lengthening shadows of the mountain peaks admonished us that it was time to return to the ship. We launched our boat, in which act we were well baptized by the waters of Crusoe's cove. We made our way back to the ship and were in time to turn to work and get the ship under way. The chain was hove short, all the sails were loosed, the bunts were dropped and sails sheeted home, the yards mast-headed, the anchor was tripped, and away we went on the home-stretch for San Francisco. As we squared away for the equator the order was given to put all sail on the ship. By eight o'clock P. M. we had every drawing sail on the ship, topgallant stun'sails and all, and she was reeling it off at about ten knots an hour.

At eight bells the watches were set, and the watch on deck was kept busy lashing the water casks. At eight bells, when the other watch came on deck, they had to take up the work where the other watch left it. And the work was continued until all the water casks were lashed, the wood stowed, and the immense gathering of fruit packed away, and everything made ship-shape again.

After we had left the island everybody on board showed an unusual buoyancy of spirits; they felt that the worst part of the tedious journey was over and that they would soon reach the goal of their ambition, there to engage in the delightful occupation of filling their pouches with glittering, shining gold.

After the passengers had recovered from the fatigue of their three days tramping and climbing on the island, they began to utilize their great store of fruits: peach pies, peach puddings, and stewed quinces were their daily fare, all prepared by themselves, as the cooks were not equal to the task of doing more than the most ordinary cooking, while we, the sailors, were well satisfied to eat the peaches in their natural condition.

March 26th, lat. 29 45 S., long. 83 06 W., wind southeast. We have now steady trade-winds and very pleasant weather; everything that can pull a pound is on the ship—stun'sails on both sides, with steady breeze right aft.

I think that the officers of the ship are throwing off that reserve which is deemed essential to the maintenance of good discipline on board of a ship. I have noticed this same disposition on board of other ships. When we were near the end of the voyage the officers would show more urbanity of manner towards the crew, although there was no laxity of necessary diciplne. As the nights were very pleasant, and the wind being dead aft, it left us nothing to do but to walk the deck. At this time, Mr. Mulroony, the second mate, threw off the reserve that appertained to his station, and unbosomed himself to me as to his plans and purposes. He told me that he was a native of Nova Scotia, and had served his apprenticeship on board of a vessel of his native province, and after he was out of his time had been promoted to the position of second mate of a ship. The captain, under whom he had served his time, urged him to stick by him, and that he would advance him to the position of chief mate as soon he could pass the necessary examination. But he said that he had become tired of going voyage after voyage to Liverpool with a ship loaded with deals. He was inspired by an ambition to see other parts of the world, and for that reason he had left his ship in Saint Johns, New Brunswick, and had gone to Boston, where, with the recommendation from the owners and captain of the ship on which he had sailed so long, he experienced no difficulty in obtaining a berth as the second mate of the ship "Vancouver," in the China trade. He had made one voyage on the ship to Hongkong, and would have continued in the ship if the California fever had not broken out, which induced him to ship on the "Urania" to go to California, and try his fortune in that golden land. He said that he had stipulated with the captain and owners that he would leave the ship when she arrived in San Francisco, from whence he intended to go the mines, and, if success should attend his efforts, he would return to his native land, Nova Scotia, where there was a sweet little cherub awaiting his return, and then they would be married and settle down in a cosy little nook, a short distance inside of Sambro lighthouse, where he could keep his boat and catch codfish and haddock, set his lobster pot, and be as grand as the governor of the Province. "Why," said he, "I found, after I came up to Boston, that the Yankees think that America begins at Old Quoddy Head, at the mouth of the Saint Croix river—that divides the United States from New Brunswick—and they think it ends in the Gulf of Mexico; but I can tell you that they are laboring under a delusion. While it is admitted, all the world over, that the people of the United States are a great people—that they produce fine mechanics, great inventors, and very enterprising merchants—they must understand that all the balance of the world is not standing still. There are the provinces of New Brunswick and Nova Scotia; they build and turn out as fine modeled and well built vessels as can be seen in the port of Liverpool to-day. I have seen the 'Ocean Monarch,' built by Donald Mac Kay, in East Boston. She was a splendid specimen of naval architecture, but I have seen just as fine in Saint Johns, New Brunswick."

March 24th. We now have a continuous steady breeze, and going along at about seven knots per hour. As we have watch and watch and have only to sway up the yards by the halyard, every twenty-four hours, it seems to us like a continuous holiday.

Every night watch on deck, unless it is my trick at the wheel or my lookout forward, the second mate comes to the waist of the ship as soon as the passengers go below, and resumes his conversation.

In speaking of ship building, he said: "The Yankees built a topsail schooner in Eastport, Maine, to run as a packet to Boston. She was a beauty, and a very fast sailer, and she was called the 'Echo.' They challenged the world to excel her. Well, without the blowing of trumpets, the 'Blue Noses,' as they call us of the Provinces, went to work and built a little full-rigged brig for the Boston trade, and called her the 'Boston.' She runs between Halifax and Boston. She looked around for the famous 'Echo.' At last they met, off the Island of Grand Menuan, both bound to Boston; wind southwest dead ahead. The race began. It was in the summer, and the wind on the New England coast during the summer season blows about southwest, with the regularity of a trade wind.

"The captain of each vessel realized that it wasn't simply a race between two fast sailing vessels, but it was between New England shipbuilders and the shipbuilders of the British Provinces. Well, sir, the 'Boston,' although a square-rigger, and having to beat to windward, right in the wind's eye, arrived in Boston eight hours before the 'Echo,' thereby proving to Brother Jonathan that while he is making long strides in ship building that the rest of the world is not standing still."

I was impressed by the remarks of the second mate. When a good man is speaking of his native country it brings out the best attributes that are in his nature. And that can truthfully be said of the people that are born under the English flag—in Gibralter, Malta, or the West Indies it is the same.

I remember that the Negroes on the Island of Barbadoes had a saying, "Queen Victoria, never fear so long as Barbadoes stand strong."

March 30th, lat. 17 31 S., long. 93 12 W. The wind during the past four days has been light and our headway has been correspondingly slow. The weather is now becoming very warm and the crew has been kept busy sewing windsails to be placed in the hatchways to cool the 'tween decks. The quarter-deck is protected by an awning, and as the wind is light, the ladies seat themselves on the trunk of the cabin and sew and knit just as if they were at home.

The contrast between the ship off Cape Horn on February 25th and her appearance March 30th is really remarkable, showing what a change in the temperature it makes between 59 06 south latitude and 17 31. Whereas February 25th was intensely cold and unpleasant, to-day, March 30th, the weather is so warm that the passengers in the 'tween-decks cabin have to be furnished with windsails to promote their comfort.

The passengers are now engaged in the pleasant task of examining their boats, of which there are several on board. Others are washing and mending their clothes in true domestic style, thereby showing their capacity to "rough it" when they reach the mines. I observe that nearly all the passengers show a degree of self-reliance that augurs well for their success in a new country.

April 4th, lat. 10 16 south, long. 94 03 west. Since we sailed from Juan Fernandez we have had an uninterrupted spell of pleasant weather, thereby verifying the fact that the Pacific Ocean is rightly named, as the word "Pacific" signifies peaceful, calm, tranquil, and such has been the state of the Pacific Ocean since we sailed from Juan Fernandez.

It reminded me of the old lady who took passage on a packet sloop that ran from Boston to Yarmouth Port, Cape Cod. As on that day the wind was fair, the crew had nothing particular to do during the passage of sixty miles distance. After she had arrived at her friend's home, the subject of a seafaring life was discussed, as nearly every man and boy on the Cape went to sea for a living. This lady, after her brief experience on the packet sloop, expressed her opinion thus: "I don't think it a hard life to go to sea, for I see that the sailors have nothing more to do than to sit around the deck and have the wind blow them along."

Such was our actual experience. During this pleasant weather, in the daytime, the crew was kept at work tarring the rigging, scraping and slushing the masts, and, as the sea was smooth, there were stagings slung over the side of the ship and we were set to work to paint ship.

In the evening Mr. Mulroony would resume his conversation on his favorite topic. "Now then," he would say, "about originality. Whoever thought of such a thing as taking logs and squaring their sides and shaping them into the form of a sailing craft, and navigating them across the Atlantic Ocean? You may think it was the Yankee, but I say it was our people; it was they that first originated the idea and carried it out to a successful issue by sailing a raft of timber across the Atlantic Ocean to Liverpool. Why," said he, "it is only lately that the Yankees have paid much attention to naval architecture. They used to buy ships from England, France, and other countries of Europe."

I interposed by saying that I had read in history that the first ship built in America was as early as the year 1616, and that it was in New York, and she was called "The Restless."

"Well," he replied, "I can't dispute that, as I don't know about it; but what is one ship? England had ships sailing to every part of the world long before that period; and to-day for one ship that you see that flies the American flag, you'll see five of England's winged messengers of trade penetrating every corner of the commercial world, and wherever you find an English merchantman you may depend on it that an English man-of-war is not far off, to protect that merchant ship, and that is what promotes England's commercial supremacy. I can tell you that England is the greatest nation in the world to foster trade and commerce, and the consequence is that England is the money center of the world."

I came to the conclusion that the progenitors of Mr. Mulroony must have been of those that left the American Colonies and settled in the British Provinces of North America, where they continued their allegiance to their beloved sovereign, King George the Third, and their descendant, who was now on board the "Urania," was imbued with the sentiments of his progenitors.

April 11th, lat. 3 06 south, long. 103 25 west. We are now near the equatorial line. To-day one of the crew asked Mr. Bardell, the amateur navigator, what was the position of the ship on this day by his reckoning. He answered that we were then in lat. 30 minutes south, right directly on the equatorial line, and long. 79 10 west.

The sailor asked Mr. Mulroony, the second mate, if he would do him the favor of pricking off that position on the chart by the divider. About one hour afterwards the second mate informed the questioner that he had examined the chart, and by measurement it placed the ship near the city of Quito, a city on the Andes Mountains about ten thousand feet above the ocean level. When Mr. Bardell was told of this he was not the least disconcerted, but answered that he had, when a boy, made a summer voyage to the Grand Bank, codfishing, as cook of a schooner, and the captain used to tell him to serve the largest doughnut and fullest turnover pie to the man that was high line at that time; and now, according to the same rule, he himself ought to be served with the best of everything on the cabin table.

After this denouement the quadrant was never brought on deck, and Mr. Scudder and Mr. Bardell turned their attention to sewing and the making of a tent of cotton drilling to shelter them in the mining regions. We had now lost the trade wind and were in the variables.

The second mate had now discontinued his night watch dissertations, as his duties required all his time. What with trimming sails, conning the helm and watching the variations in the wind and weather, he was kept on the *qui vive* during every watch after this until we arrived in San Francisco, after which time I never saw him again.

The wind was now light and baffling, veering all round the compass, and the heat was oppressive. The effect upon the passengers was quite apparent; dullness and lassitude seemed to pervade the whole ship.

April 14th, lat. 2 08 north, long. 104 16 west. The wind is very light, while the heat is very oppressive. To-day an affair happened which at most any other time would have been attended with fatal results.

MAN FALLS OVERBOARD.

There was among the passengers a gentleman somewhat advanced in years, and accompanied by two of his sons, young and active men. I was informed that he was from some town in Worcester county, Mass., and his name was Boutwell. He was a gentleman of education, and owned a fine farm and was in affluent circumstances at home. But like thousands of other men who never seem to know when they have enough of this world's goods, he had left his home to participate in the general scramble for wealth. He was a studious man, and for that reason I had only seen him on deck three or four times from the time that I came on board the ship in Rio de Janeiro. On this day it was our forenoon watch on deck. We were engaged in our work of cleaning and painting, when, about six bells, the fearful cry rang out loud, "Man overboard! man overboard!" As the passengers were most all on deck at the time the confusion that ensued was embarrassing. The crew jumped for the starboard quarter boat and soon had it in the water. As the wind was very light and the sea very smooth, the crew soon got away from the ship and grasped the drowning man before he sunk for the last time, and took him in the boat and returned to the ship. All this time the ship had been brought up to the wind and the yards hove aback. After the rescued man had been taken on deck he proved to be Mr. Boutwell.

It seems that he had been reading the Holy Bible with unusual earnestness and had conceived in his mind that he was inspired by faith equal to that of Abraham when he went up into the mountain to offer his son Isaac as a sacrifice. On that day he put his faith to a practical test, and the result was a lamentable failure, for when he essayed to walk on the water he soon found himself sinking, the same as any other man that didn't possess any extraordinary degree of sanctity.

After this voluntary bath in the broad Pacific, Capt. Buckland enjoined on his two sons the absolute necessity of guarding their father incessantly until the ship should arrive in San Francisco.

I think I did not see him again while I was on board the ship. This occurrence caused considerable talk among the passengers about the cupidity of men who already possess an abundance of wealth and yet are ready to risk their precious necks in the scramble for more.

April 15th, lat. 9 45 north, long. 112 06 west. The wind is very light and the weather is hot. The windsails leading below the hatches give a mouthful of air to the passengers, but as we have nothing of that kind leading down into the forecastle it is as hot as an oven down there.

As the weather is pleasant many of the passengers have brought up their blankets and picked out spots on top of the water casks where they pass the night.

April 20th. A young man named Conkling, a native of Pittsfield, Mass., has become so seriously affected by the heat that he has become a simpleton and incapable of taking care of himself. It seems that he had become so careless about himself that his fellow-passengers hustled him out of the 'tween decks and forced him on deck. When the captain investigated the matter he ordered some of the crew to take the young man in hand and to care for him. When the men were putting clean clothes upon the poor, simple, good-natured fellow, they found a belt upon his person which was opened in the presence of the captain and was found to contain five hundred dollars in gold coin, in five and ten dollar pieces. This money was turned over to the captain's care, to be returned to the young man when the ship arrived in San Francisco. Clean washing and clean clothes had a very beneficial effect upon him and in a measure restored his faculties.

As I have said before the "Urania" carried a very large longboat turned over on top of the forward house, and the bow of the boat projected over the house some two feet to the foremast, which enabled a person to go up under the boat, where he had ample room.

By direction of the mate what dunnage was stowed away under the longboat was taken out and a clean bed with clean bedding was arranged by the crew, which became the stateroom of Mr. Conkling until the ship arrived in San Francisco.

April 22d. We now have the wind south-southwest and everything is on the ship, and the sea being as smooth as a millpond she is making latitude very rapidly. By observation at noon our latitude was 15 03 north, long. 119 25 west. We now have the prospect of arriving at our port of destination in a short time, and the passengers are now preparing to invade an unknown country, where they expect to encounter Indians and wild beasts.

The deck is looking like a veritable arsenal. Guns, pistols, bowie-knives, powder flasks, and other death-dealing apparatus that a man may need in a new, unexplored country, can now be seen in the process of being cleaned and prepared for action when needed.

Young Conkling, in his new quarters under the longboat, is quite contented and is gaining in flesh. He is constantly around the sailors, seeming to look upon them as his only friends. The case of this young man is really a sad one, and as I heard it, it excited my commiseration. I was informed that he was the youngest of three brothers in Berkshire county, Mass., who had inherited a patrimony of a fine farm and a large tract of wood land near Pittsfield. They labored on their farm during the summer and chopped wood during the winter, which they marketed in the neighboring town the ensuing fall. And thus they would have remained satisfied but for the California fever which swept all New England like a whirlwind. The brothers resolved to make a venture by sending the youngest brother, as did the ancient Israelites, "to spy out the land." The bountiful manner in which the young man had been fitted out gave proof of how well they had performed their task and their ability to do so. Their impatience to become suddenly very rich is proof that man is always reaching for that which is unattainable on earth—that is, perfect, unalloyed felicity.

April 25th, lat. 21 15 north, long. 114 05 west. We are now looking for and longing for the day which we now think is near, when we shall be set free from this ship, the same as a lot of imprisoned birds are released from an aviary. We sight vessels now nearly every day. We now can see that we are nearing the focus of our hopes and anticipations.

April 28th, lat. 30 12 north, long. 119 06 west. We are now reaching for our long expected central point, San Francisco, in lat. 37 47 55 north, long. 122 24 52 west.

We now have a spanking breeze abeam, and this ship

shows her best speed with the wind abeam. Every man on board appears to labor under unusual excitement, and all seem to be nervous and eager to know how fast the ship is going through the water.

At eight bells the mate sung out, "Heave the log!" "Aye, aye, sir," answered the men, and while one of them fetched the logline twenty or more of the passengers came trooping aft to ascertain the speed of the ship. When the line had been run out, the mate announced the speed as "nine knots."

As I had the first trick at the wheel during the first watch that night Capt. Buckland, who was walking on the weather side of the quarter-deck, approached the binnacle, looked into the compass, and as he stood there he addressed me for the first time since I had been on board the ship: " Well, young man, how do you like the change in ships that you have made?" "I like it very much, sir, I thank you; and furthermore, sir, I shall never forget your kindness in having given me a berth on board this ship." "As to that," said he, " by what my officers tell me, I think that you have earned your passage; but I advise you in the future not to put yourself in a position in a foreign port, nor in any other port, where you will have to beg your passage. Had it not been that your acquaintance had recommended you as being a respectable man, I would not have allowed you to come on board my ship, for my experience has taught me to beware of beach-combers in South American ports." By speaking thus of beach-combers, Capt. Buckland was alluding to abandoned, dissolute sailors, that either run away or are driven away from ships, particularly whaleships, because they are evil-disposed mischief breeders, and are called beach-combers because while they are ashore they work on board of lighters, unloading cargoes from the ships in the harbors where there are no wharves. That was the only time that Capt. Buckland ever spoke to me, for after the ship arrived in San Francisco I never met him; but as I said before, while he was a man of few words he was a kind hearted gentleman.

April 30th, lat. 32 49 north, long. 120 03 west. The fair weather has left us and we have the wind about west-northwest and hazy weather. The ship now looks trim and shapely, as the topmasts and topgallant and royalmasts have all been scraped and slushed, the bulwarks painted inside and out, as well as the bends of the ship. The boats were all painted on the inside and on the outside. In fact, I think there was more work done on the "Urania," in watch and watch, than there would have been if all hands had been kept on deck during the afternoons after we got into pleasant weather.

The steward and the cooks seemed to feel the necessity of conciliating the crew when we were so near to the end of the voyage, and they prepared for us a treat that I had not partaken of since I had joined the "Urania." We were regaled with dried apple pies one day this week, and to-night, for our supper, they passed to us out of the galley a tin pan heaping full of doughnuts.

May 2d, lat. 35 09 north, long. 121 16 west. We are now, all of us, on the tenter hooks of expectation.

To-day we have sighted five vessels, all of them steering in the same direction as ourselves.

This night the mates ordered that two men should take a lookout station on the topgallant forecastle, one on the weather bow and one on the lee bow. We had the middle watch on this night, and it seemed a short watch because of the passengers, who tramped around the decks all night long. Every half hour some one of them would come forward and hail with, "Say, do you see anything?" "No, sir," I would answer, "only the light from the vessel on our lee quarter."

When the larboard watch was called at four A. M. and we were relieved we left a number of passengers on deck who had not turned in during the night.

When our watch was called at seven bells we received from the galley for breakfast that which astonished our stomachs; it was nothing less than fried ham and boiled rice. This fare was unprecedented. We hadn't seen anything of the kind since we left Rio, and the members of the crew told me that it was the first time that fried ham had been passed into the forecastle since the ship left Boston.

May 3d. By observation at noon our position was lat. 37 03 north, long. 122 50 west.

After the captain had examined his chart, which he placed on the capstan, and pricked off the position of the ship, he told the mate to send a man aloft to the foretopmast crosstrees to keep a sharp lookout for land. When the passengers heard this order they were in a tremor of excitement, and some of the youngest of them made an attempt to go aloft, but the mate quickly checked their ardor, for when we left Rio the captain had given strict orders to the two mates not to permit any of the passengers to go into the rigging, as it might result in a catastrophe, and it is a very proper rule on board of a passenger ship. Vessels were quite numerous on both sides of our ship, but quite a distance off.

About four P. M. we sighted a ship standing to the southward which the mate said had come out from San Francisco.

About five P. M. the lookout aloft gave the joyful news of "Land ho!" "Where away?" asked the captain. "Four points on the weather bow, sir." "Very well; come down." The lookout came down on deck, and when the captain had gone aloft with his spyglass and scanned the land, he returned on deck and said it was a group of rocky islands called the Farallones, in lat. 37 41 north, long. 123 01 west, about twenty-five miles southwest from San Francisco harbor.

At this announcement the passengers became almost uncontrollable with glee. A number of them struck up the favorite refrain:

"Oh, Susannah, don't you cry for me;
I'm going to California with my washbowl on my knee."

As we approached near to the rocky, craggy, barren-looking island we could see myriads of birds circling around on the wing, which we afterwards learned made these rocky islands their breeding place, and from whence San Francisco was supplied with an abundance of eggs during the months of June and July.

At seven P. M. the captain ordered all light sails to be taken in and to put the ship under topsails, foresail, jib and spanker. We then hauled off and lay off and on during the night. The wind was to the westward and the weather clear. The passengers were nearly all of them on deck, gathered in groups and engaged in merry conversation.

The night passed, and at four A. M. the captain came on deck and ordered the ship to be put on her course for the harbor and all sail to be made on her. When the watch was called all hands were ordered to make sail on the ship. We scrambled aloft with light hearts and loosed the topgallantsails and royals for the last time on board the "Urania." Everything was set by five A. M., and the watch was ordered below for the last time.

At seven bells, when the watch was called, the land on the larboard hand was plainly in sight and the ship was heading about northeast.

On this morning all hands forward sat to their first and last breakfast together, as before this we had eaten our breakfasts watch and watch.

Directly after breakfast we were ordered to get the leadline and a man was lashed outside the forechains to heave the lead. At that time ships that entered the harbor of San Francisco had to be guided by lead and line, as there were no pilots, nor were the shoals and rocks indicated by buoys.

Well, as the sailors call it, we felt our way along until we came up to the bar. As we approached it the captain, who had gone aloft onto the foreyard with his spyglass, conned the wheel and directed the trimming of the sails.

As the ship approached the land, on the larboard hand the green hills and deep valleys of the Marin shore came into full view, gladdening the eyes of every person on board. The ladies had stationed themselves on the trunk of the cabin, and were as smartly dressed as if they expected company.

As we approached Lime Point, on our larboard hand the beautiful green hills, with numerous cattle, that looked at that distance like so many lambs, and the umbrageous trees of live oak, with outspreading branches, brought to mind the old English song of spring-time:

> " Our eyes were bright, our hearts were light,
> And nature's face was gay;
> The trees their leafy branches spread,
> And perfumes filled sweet May.
> 'Twas there we heard the cuckoo's note
> Steal softly through the air,
> While everything around us looked
> Most charming, sweet and fair."

On our starboard bow we saw a bluff jutting into the bay on the apex of which were to be seen two or three small brass cannon. Rising far above the cannon was a tall flagstaff from the top of which waved the glorious flag of our country. At the sight of the flag, one of the young passengers called out: "Look, boys! Look at the banner of our dear country. After having sailed more than eighteen thousand miles over two vast oceans, that flag tells us that we are about to place our feet on the soil of our beloved country—the land of the brave and the home of the free." As he uttered these words he jumped upon the topgallant forecastle and recited the following lines from Drake's Ode to the American Flag:

> " Forever float that standard sheet;
> Where breathes the foe but falls before us,
> With freedom's soil beneath our feet,
> And freedom's banner waving o'er us?"

At the conclusion of the recital all hands gave three cheers for the American flag.

Next came into view the whitewashed adobe walls and tiled roofs of the Presidio barracks, with its sloping verdant lawn. On our larboard side was Alcatraz, which in Spanish signifies pelican, as this small rocky island was the home of the pelican, that preyed upon the fish in the bay. Before us loomed Telegraph Hill, which was already surmounted by a small wooden house, through the center of which shot up into space a mast about fifty feet high from which projected arms according to the wishes of its manager, thus: For a schooner just coming into port he would hoist one arm; for a brig, two arms; for a ship three arms, thus:

In this way, as soon as the man on guard with his telescope descried a vessel in the offing, he would raise arms from the mast according to the rig of the vessel. Hence the name Telegraph Hill.

The mate now called out, "Take in the royals. Take in the topgallantsails. Haul up the mainsail and unhook the tacks and sheets. Haul down the flying jib."

As we sailed into view of the harbor our eyes were greeted with a sight that they never have encountered since. Shipping in such numbers that it was absolutely impossible to enumerate them; they seemed and looked to us as we were entering the harbor as if they were piled up one on top of the other. I will here enumerate some of the vessels whose names I a few days afterward took pains to learn: The very first vessel I saw at anchor was the French ship "Chataubriand," of Havre; the "Thomas Bennett," of Charleston, S. C.; "Salem," of New York; "Genessee;" the "Callao;" the "Izetto;" "Sarah Parker," of Nantucket; "Friendship," of Edgartown, Mass.; the "John Jay;" the "Mary," of Nantucket; the "Cadmus;" the "Deucalion;" "Morrison," of Philadelphia; "Ganges," of Gloucester, Mass.; "Carib," of Salem; "Palladium," of Boston; "Dianthe," of Boston. "Samuel Russell," of New York; the "Albany" and the "Utica," of New York; schooner "John Allyne," of New Bedford; pilot boat "Favorite," of New Bedford; sloop "Burr,"—came through the Straits of Magellan; schooner "Osceola," of New Bedford; bark "Eureka," of Cleveland, Ohio; schr. "Horace," from New Bedford; schooner "A. Emery," of Berwick, Me.; brigs "Ark," and "James Caskie," two deckers, of Newburyport, Mass.; "South America," and the ' ?hrnia Providence, R. I.; "Niantic," of Warren, R. I.; .i &r \ rison," and if I could remember them all it would in. book to enumerate them.

When we got abreast of Yerba Buena Island, now called Goat Island, we hauled up to the southward and westward and skirted the closely anchored shipping and dropped our anchor in the harbor near Rincon Point, San Francisco, lat. 37 47 55 north, long. 122 24 52 west.

As we dropped our anchor and heard the chain run out we all felt that we would never again sail another foot on the ship "Urania," nor any other, unless it would be as a first-class cabin passenger.

We went aloft and furled all the sails snug and took good care to put an artistic bunt on each one of the square sails. After the sails were furled and the decks were cleared up, the mate, Mr. Ingraham, called Tom and myself to him and told us that we were released from further service on board the "Urania." It being now six o'clock I resolved to pass one more night on board.

Of the ships mentioned as being in the harbor of San Francisco, very few of them ever went out of the harbor again. The most of them were turned into storeships, by having large sections cut out of their sides level with the 'tween decks, and thus they were utilized as storeships where goods were placed on board from other ships, and then taken ashore to the beach in lighters as they were needed.

Some of these ships had a very interesting history. There was the "John Jay," that took Benjamin Franklin to France as American Embassador in 1776.

There was the "Cadmus," on board which ship Gen. Lafayette made his voyage to the United States in 1824.

There was the schooner "John Allyne," that was bought, fitted out and loaded by a company of intending miners. After they arrived off Cape Horn they resolved to sail through the Straits of Magellan, and when they were going through they anchored in one of the numerous bays and sent their boats ashore to obtain a supus / of wood and water. Of those that went ashore was a man named Benjamin Franklin Bourne, of Buzzard's Bay, Mass., in honor of whose family the recently incorporated town of Bourne, on Cape Cod, where President Cleveland has his summer home, is named. Well, as they had about got through with the labor of wood gathering, they espied a formidable number of Patagonian Indians coming down the cliffs towards them. The crew at once made for their boats and shoved off, but they discovered that Mr. Bourne was not among them. Being seized with fear and not knowing but what the Indians might board the schooner and capture them all, they returned to the vessel and got under way, and left Mr. Bourne to his fate. This was in the beginning of 1849. The vessel got through the straits all safe and after a safe passage they put into Valparaiso in order to send the news to Mr. Bourne's friends of the sad fate of the gentleman. The news arrived in Boston in the latter part of June. President Taylor died in July, and was succeeded by Millard Fillmore. The new President appointed Daniel Webster, who was an old friend of the Bourne family, as Secretary of State. Mr. Benj. F. Bourne, Sr., went to Mr. Webster, and the result was that the Secretary of the Navy ordered the sloop-of-war "Vandalia," that was at that time being fitted out for the Pacific station, to sail through the Straits of Magellan and make search at every available point for the missing gentleman. In the meantime another schooner went through the straits, some six months after the capture, and the Patagonians brought Mr. Bourne to the place where she had anchored to get wood and water. As they showed a disposition to release their prisoner, the captain of the schooner gave them sufficient of such articles as he had and which they desired, and the prisoner, Mr. Bourne, was yielded up into the hands of his countryman. The sufferings and abuses which the gentleman suffered at the hands of the giant Patagonians were such that the relation of them would melt a heart of stone. The "Vandalia" obeyed the orders of the Secretary of the Navy, but she had been forestalled in her errand of mercy. This was the history of the "John Allyne." Mr. Bourne was brought to California on board the schooner that received him, and in due time returned to New Bedford and afterwards became a rich man by his enterprise at home.

The schooner "Osceola," which vessel was mentioned with others, had her history. The Boston and Sandwich Glass Company needed a vessel to run between Boston and Sandwich, Cape Cod, to carry material to the glass works and bring to Boston the manufactured glass. They had one vessel, but needed another that would draw less water. They found a vessel in New Haven, Conn. She was a sloop named the "Osceola," built on Long Island Sound to run between New Haven and Albany, N. Y. She was sharp as a wedge forward, with a fine clean run, and flat on the floor as a house. She had a center-board and drew but little water, which was the desideratum, because Sandwich harbor has a sandbar at the mouth of it. She was bought in New Haven and a captain and crew were sent to bring her to Boston by the way of Nantucket Shoals and around the Highlands of Cape Cod. When the captain saw the sloop, and examined her model, he refused to bring her around to Boston—because it was November and a gale of wind might set in—and another and more courageous captain had to be sent. She was brought around Cape Cod safely and into Boston. She was run between Boston and Sandwich for a number of years, until the Old Colony Railroad was built and a branch was extended to Sandwich. This obviated the necessity for keeping the "Osceola" running, and she was offered for sale in the early part of the year 1849. A company from New Bedford bought her, and took her over the shoals and through Wood's Hole into Buzzard's Bay, to New Bedford. There she was fitted out, the center-board was secured in the well, and a false keel put on her. She sailed for California, and when she encountered the first gale of wind in the Gulf Stream, she slatted her mast right out of her, breaking it off near the deck. A jurymast was fitted up and she made her way back to New Bedford, was rigged into a schooner and started again, and came to California safe and sound and run on this coast for many years afterwards. Now, when I compare the achievement of these intrepid men with the doings of Columbus and his fellow-voyagers on the vessels "Santa Maria" and the "Pinta," I don't know which of them most to admire, for Columbus, after a period of thirty or forty days at the longest, intended to return to the port of Palos, in Spain, from whence he started; but these adventurous descendants of the Puritans knew to a certainty that a perilous journey was before them, over two trackless oceans, which would last six or eight months in length.

The "Niantic" was afterwards filled in just where she lay, and now the spot forms the northwest corner of Clay and Sansome streets, which locality is to-day six wide business streets distant from the margin of the bay.

After a night's rest, not having a watch to stand, I arose early the next morning and after breakfast I went ashore with others in the longboat, and about nine o'clock I placed my feet on the shores of the new El Dorado, the place that had absorbed all my thoughts and on which I had centered my fondest anticipations—the goal of my ambition, where I hoped that I would at least be able to earn a comfortable living without being obliged to any longer follow the sea, after having done so for the past fourteen years of my life.

We landed near Rincon Point, from whence we had to make a long circuit to reach the town, for from where Folsom and East streets intersect now to First street it was all bay, with ships of the largest class riding at anchor thereon. One of them, the "Callao," lies to-day on the very spot where she rode at anchor at that time. It is now called Beale street, between Mission and Howard streets, and there are Main, Spear, Steuart and East streets between where the ship is buried in the street and the water front of to-day.

As I walked around the margin of the bay I found myself in a town of tents. I saw but very few houses, and those that I did see were small buildings that had been framed in the Eastern States and sent around Cape Horn on board of ships.

When I reached First street—and the reason why it was called First street is because it then was the first street on the margin of the bay, although to-day it is seven wide streets removed from the bay—when I reached First street, between Mission and Minna, there was a little steamer of about one hundred and fifty tons being put together. She had been constructed in the East and every part numbered and marked, then taken apart and put on board of a ship and brought out here and reconstructed. When she was completed she was named the "Sagamore." Her career was very brief, for she was blown up the following September.

As I walked up the beach I noticed that every man that I saw appeared to be busy as a bee. They worked as though they had much to do and but little time to do it in.

When I arrived where California and Sansome streets now intersect, and which was then the beach, I found a man there with a team of two mustang horses and a wagon, loading some brick which had been discharged from a lighter. I accosted him with the usual salutation of "Good morning, sir." He answered pleasantly, "Good morning." I said, "I have just arrived here in a ship, and would like to help you to load those bricks." "Well," said he, "you are not dressed for this kind of work." "Well, sir," I replied, "I dont care about my clothes, for I've got more clothes than money." "If that is your condition," said he, "you may take right hold," and I did. After the wagon was loaded he took the load up California street, just above Montgomery, where they were building a house for a firm named Fitzgerald, Bausch & Brewster. After he had dumped the brick he returned, and I had taken bricks enough out of the water to load the wagon again. We loaded three loads in about two hours, when the job was finished. He asked me how much I wanted. I answered that I would take what he had a mind to give me. He then put his hand into his pocket and pulled out a two dollars and a half gold piece. I thanked him most sincerely, and I felt then as if I had really reached a land that was "flowing with milk and honey," and thank

God for His goodness, I have never had reason to change my mind. Just then the following lines by Charles Mackay came to my mind:

" A willing heart and a ready hand
    Are priceless to the young,
And are the sources whence success
    In every age has sprung;
Then cherish them, ye noble lads,
    Whatever may assail,
For a willing heart and a ready hand
    Are never known to fail."

FINIS.

The following lines, which I wrote on July 4th, 1876, and which express the inmost feelings of my heart, I now publish in addition to the story of my trip to California:

OUR CENTENNIAL BIRTHDAY.

The day made glorious on the western main,
   From which sweet Freedom takes its yearly date,
Now dawns with brightness on the land again,
   Where grateful millions guide its onward fate.

Oppression's bonds their early years confined;
   Slaves in the cherished land that gave them birth;
Each man resolved with firm, unwavering mind,
   To strike a blow to free his home and hearth.

Ruled by a king enthroned 'mid distant seas,
   Deaf to appeals borne from this western shore,
He aimed with stern, unstatesmanlike decrees,
   To claim for tribute all their humble store.

The royal tyrant, with outrageous laws,
   Essayed to crush the honest sons of toil;
In vain did Justice plead the sufferer's cause,
   Nor Mercy's tears could stay the hand of spoil.

The issue forced upon unwilling hands,
   That ne'er did wish from parent ties to part,
'Till royal greed, with its unjust demands,
   Drove loyalty from each indignant heart.

The day on which the deadly strife began
   Gave birth to a nation that ignores a king;
Its limits reach towards the setting sun;
   Two mighty oceans to its borders cling.

One century marks her course of self-control,
   And lo! behold her now, a mighty nation;
Unnumbered ships her starry flag unfold—
   The brightest banner that illumes creation.

What heart but beats on this Centennial day
   With conscious dignity, nor swells with pride;
What lips but breathe sweet Freedom's sacred lay,
   That gives man all—earth can give naught beside.

Perish the hand that basely lifts the sword,
   This land, that patriots won, to sever;
Cursed be the tongue that would with trait'rous word
   Soil her flag, whose folds shall wave forever.

America! safe haven for down-trodden man,
   Elysium of industrious, happy throngs.
Praise the brave founders of thy freedom's plan,
   To them the honor of this day belongs.

www.ingramcontent.com/pod-product-compliance
Lightning Source LLC
Chambersburg PA
CBHW032226230426
43666CB00033B/1605